PASTERNAK
a pictorial biography

BY GERD RUGE

THAMES AND HUDSON · LONDON

Boris Pasternak has lived through an epoch which has been both great and terrifying, an age of fiery emotions and of cold abstractions. World-shaking events have followed each other in rapid succession—wars, revolutions, five-year-plans, purges—all of them glorious, all of them horrible. How could the poet, in an age convulsed as this one was by such far-reaching events, hope to leave his mark except by struggling to rediscover the broad, untrammelled path which man is destined through all adversity to follow?

Faced by such a task his personal life fades into insignificance. He is not a man of action who forces events and stimulates developments. The milestones which mark the various stages of his life are the years that saw the birth of his literary products and the publication dates of his books. From his writings and from statements made by his friends we can see the rough outlines of a man who stepped from a youth spent in a milieu as Russian as it was European on to a building-site where revolutionary engineers were trying to construct the man and the universe of the future. The prevailing circumstances do not allow us to connect up all the countless small links into a complete chronological chain of events. Boris Pasternak drew his creative strength from his personal experience, yet it seems that he never wrote about his private affairs. Even in his autobiographical notes there is no chronological sequence of events, nor did he try to reconstruct them from his memories. Of his first autobiographical attempt he says, 'I am not writing my autobiography. Like the leading character (of this work) I too think that only heroes deserve a real biography, but the life story of a poet cannot be presented in this form! The poet gives such a consciously steep upward curve to the whole course of his life that it cannot possibly exist on the vertical line of a biography, where we would expect to find it.' But one thing we can do—we can sketch in the background against which he lives and creates. We can show how much, or how little, he was moulded by his surroundings and the events of his time.

The Pasternak children a
their parents' Silver Wedding
(1914). From left to right
Boris, reciting a poem, Josephine
Lydia and Alexander. (From a
painting by Leonid Pasternak)
▶

Boris Pasternak's parents—the
painter, Leonid Pasternak, and
his pianist wife, Rosa
Kaufman-Pasternak. (From a
painting by Leonid Pasternak)

Friends of his family said, 'Boris Pasternak has his father's genius multiplied by that of his mother', and, indeed, from all that is known about his parents it becomes clear how happy the early years of his life must have been. He grew up in an atmosphere where the love of music and painting predominated. His early poems and prose have been said to reflect the technique of the impressionist painters, yet it seems unjust to forget the part which music played in his development. But what is perhaps more important is the fact that music as well as painting were to his parents not hobbies but serious creative work. His father, Leonid Pasternak, was one of the best-known Russian painters and art teachers of his time. His mother, Rosa Kaufman-Pasternak, gave up a brilliant career as a concert pianist to devote herself whole-heartedly to her family and to her husband. A portrait of Boris Pasternak would be incomplete without a brief outline of the remarkable parents of this remarkable man.

Rosa Kaufman-Pasternak, daughter of a wealthy soda-water manufacturer, was born in Odessa in 1867. Already as a child she manifested her great musical talent by teaching herself to play the piano. She was given lessons, and at the age of ten gave her first recitals. Her success in Odessa was considerable. Serious critics wrote about her performances, and well-known musicians undertook her musical education. At the age of thirteen, having performed in many Russian towns, she came to the notice of the celebrated pianist Anton Rubinstein who arranged concerts for her in Moscow and St Petersburg, which at that time were the centres of the musical world. A serious illness interrupted her work, but soon she was again giving concerts in Russia, Poland and, finally, in Vienna; it was in the Austrian capital that the young pianist, who in the meantime had outgrown the role of infant prodigy, completed her training. During the 'eighties, having returned to the Conservatoire of Music in Odessa as a piano teacher, she met the young painter, Leonid Pasternak. In 1889 they married.

Leonid Pasternak was also born in Odessa—five years earlier than Rosa Kaufman. Life in Odessa was at that time rich and colourful as in few other towns in the world. Ships from many lands crowded its port. Its population was a lively polyglot mixture of Greeks, Russians, Ukrainians, Caucasians and Jews; but it was the Jewish community which then and in the years following produced an unbelievably large number of talented people, people who even now play an important role in the literary and musical life of Russia and of the world. The Odessa of that time was a gay cosmopolitan town whose upper classes were exceptionally cultured people with strong artistic leanings. Odessa boasted of having the finest opera house east of Vienna, and for many of its people Vienna seemed no more distant than Moscow. The Odessa in which Boris Pasternak's parents grew up was quite another thing from the remote coastal town that it is today.

Leonid Pasternak's early love for painting was encouraged and deepened by friends of his family, but his father felt it might be better for the boy to learn something more practical. So he sent his son to Moscow to study medicine at the university there; but here temptation loomed in the shape of the School of Painting, Sculpture and Architecture—and he could not quite resist its siren song. He saved and worked in order to be able to go to the art school, but just as he seemed about to reach his goal fate intervened, causing him to turn his attention elsewhere. It was more or less by chance that he found himself bound for Munich, which in those days was known as the 'Athens on the Isar' and which attracted disciples of art from all over the world. There the professors taught him the art of painting. Nevertheless, on his return to Moscow his life was by no means one of ease and security. To begin with he did drawings for magazines and success came very slowly. This was roughly the time of his first meeting with his future wife, who gave up her career as concert pianist to subordinate her interests to those of her husband.

Boris Pasternak at the age of eight. A drawing by his father, Leonid Pasternak (1898)

The first child of the young married couple was Boris, born in 1890 in Arsenal Street in Moscow in one of the single-storeyed houses that were so typical of the old part of the town. As it was a house built of stone and not of timber, it was one of the more prosperous-looking buildings; nevertheless the windows of Leonid Pasternak's flat looked out on to the archway through which the carriages with their drivers rattled into the courtyard. This part of the town was full of bustle and colour but it was not exactly the smartest district of

The composer, Sergei
Rachmaninov, was one of
the closest friends of
Leonid Pasternak

Moscow. In those days it was easier for a Russian citizen to study in Vienna or in Munich. In Moscow the artist was not a privileged person and it was difficult for a young painter to make the grade however talented he might be.

But Leonid Pasternak was the kind of person who does succeed. Remembering his years of study in Munich, he tried his hand as a teacher in a private art school. This provided the necessities of life for his family, and at the same time he worked as a free-lance artist. Through his work he met painters, musicians and writers; he painted the portraits of Rachmaninov, Scriabin and Rubinstein; he met Leo Tolstoy and illustrated his novel, *War and Peace*. In 1893 he was asked to join the staff of the Moscow School of Painting,

The composer, Alexander Scriabin, Boris Pasternak's music teacher. (Drawing by Leonid Pasternak)

Sculpture and Architecture, and young Boris Pasternak moved with his parents into the Principal's flat. In the beautiful building in Mjasnitzkij Street the boy met the intellectuals and artists of the Russia of that time, whose names meant little to him then but whose way of life and behaviour created the atmosphere in which he grew up. Here art was a normal activity which needed neither explanation nor apology and which could fill out and take possession of a man's whole life.

If Rosa Pasternak rarely made an appearance in the great concert halls, she played often in the circle of her friends. One of the men in this circle was Leo Tolstoy who welcomed the Pasternaks in Yasnaya Polyana and often visited them in town. In 1894 Rosa and two

professors of the Moscow Conservatoire gave a concert in her home. The crying of the four-year-old Boris, awakened by the music of the trio, called his mother away from the piano to his bedside. Nearly sixty years later he recalls this incident. 'It seems likely', he recalls, 'that they carried me in so that I should see the guests, or perhaps I was looking through the frame of the open door into the salon. The room was in a cloud of smoke. The candles blinked as if the smoke hurt their eyes. They played glittering scales of light on the polished mahogany of the violin and the 'cello. The piano was black and so were the suits of the men. The necks and shoulders of the ladies rose out of their low-cut dresses like flowers out of a festal bouquet. The smoke rings blended with the grey hair of two or three elderly people.' Among the grey-haired guests whom the young Boris was to remember well was Leo Tolstoy. Of Tolstoy he says, 'His spirit pervaded our whole house.'

It is in this world in which music ever sounded, this world of art and artists, that Boris Pasternak grew up. Around him the expanding Moscow of the foundation years was smothering the picturesque old town. Towering over the wooden houses with their meticulously carved façades rose new buildings, often overladen with ornament. Although in streets surmounted by countless glittering church spires the coachmen still wore their colourful dress, the growth of the ancient capital of Russia followed impetuously that of western towns. Moscow, which for years had led a sleepy existence in the shadow of that

Leo Tolstoy, a friend of the Pasternaks,
in conversation (left) and working on the land (right).
(Drawings by Leonid Pasternak)

elegant, erudite and sparkling town of the Tsars, St Petersburg, was bursting its seams with energy and enterprise. To the ambitious plans of the rising industrialists the brittle remnants of a rigid feudal system were a source of irritation. The writers with their new ideas came into conflict with the official censor and the Church. Russia's art, trying to come to terms with an era of great change, experienced a renaissance. Cleaving to the strong and glowing colours of an almost rural past, yet stimulating and brimful with energy—this was young Boris Pasternak's world.

At the age of ten the young Boris went through an experience which later was to have an inexplicably deep influence on him and his attitude to poetry. It was the meeting with Rainer Maria Rilke. Thirty years later Pasternak wrote, 'On a hot summer's morning in the year 1900 an express train left the Kursk station in Moscow. Just before the train was due to leave a man in a black Tyrolean cape came to the window of our compartment; with him was a tall woman who might have been his mother or his elder sister. Both conversed with my father on a subject to which they all three applied themselves with equal warmth. The woman now and then exchanged a few words in Russian with my mother; the stranger spoke only German. Although I knew that language well I had never heard it spoken in such a way before, and it was for that reason that this man in the bustle on the platform between the first and second bells appeared to me like a silhouette in the midst of solid bodies, a fiction in a thicket of reality.'

It was not until two or three years later, while putting his father's books in order, that the sensitive and impressionable boy found a book which he carried with him for a long time—a volume of poems by Rilke, *Mir zur Feier*. The magic of the poetry did not escape him, for in his home German was spoken often and with enthusiasm. Young Boris had even been prepared by his mother and private tutors for a German school in Moscow, although in 1901 he actually became a second-year pupil of the Moscow grammar school No. 5. But the lively, polemic and creative world of his father's artistic friends did far more to shape Boris Pasternak's life than his formal education. This was a world which owed its inner tranquillity to his mother's self-sacrificing renunciation of her own brilliant career. The air which Boris, his brother Alexander and his sisters Josephine and Lydia were breathing was saturated with music. It was therefore quite natural that the eldest son should be given piano lessons; but it was when the twelve-year-old Boris met Alexander Scriabin that his liking for music grew into an overwhelming passion.

This great composer with his strangely fascinating personality was the neighbour from whose house mysteriously intoxicating chords drifted across the wood to the house near Obolenskoje which Leonid Pasternak had rented for the summer. And just in the same way as he had done after the meeting with Rilke, Boris found himself strangely enchanted. In those years it seemed that fate intended him to become a musician. Six years later the

Rainer Maria Rilke in Moscow
(Painting by Leonid Pasternak)

same Alexander Scriabin, his idol, was to take this enchantment from him. Pasternak says of himself during those days, 'I loved music more than anything and Scriabin more than anyone in the world of music.' A life divorced from music seemed to him inconceivable, and even after the union of music and literature in his life Scriabin's spirit left his imprint on Pasternak's poems for a long time—not as the musical element which pervades all his poetry, but even more as the spirit of aesthetic experiment which seeks to combine sound and colour, philosophy and religious feeling, meditation and the awareness of nature in a single work.

At the turn of the century Leonid Pasternak travelled twice to Paris, where the exhibitions of the French Impressionists inspired and encouraged him in his work. Without sacrificing the clean forceful contours which were the result of his fine draughtsmanship, he joined the ranks of the new school of the open-air painters whose works at this time belonged to the best that secular painting in Russia has produced. It was during those years that he painted his beautiful landscapes—delicate and rich with atmosphere, full of life and not at all academic. In Obolenskoje he painted his 'Meadow at Night'.

One day some young girls from a neighbouring village were riding after a herd of horses and the young Boris Pasternak decided to gallop after them on horseback. Jumping a brook, he was thrown and broke his leg. To this day it has remained a trifle shorter than the other, and after nearly sixty years this injury still compels him to stand at a high desk while working.

The sensitive seismographs of literature even in those years gave clear signs of the severe earthquakes that were to come. The classic period of the Russian novel came to an end, giving way to a decade of symbolists, the first decade of a quarter-century in which lyrical poetry dominated Russian literature. Realism in prose had sunk to a level of plain mediocrity; only Anton Chekhov, Ivan Bunin and Maxim Gorky kept up a high standard, each in his own individual way. The revolution in the field of art which led to a revaluation and reversal of artistic tenets in Western Europe took place in Russia also. The awakening individualism expressed itself in true Russian fashion in the currents of intellectual life in St Petersburg and Moscow, and all the various literary streams flowed together in the Symbolism which marked the beginning of the Russian literature of our century, and which gave to it its main impetus. Alexander Blok, Vyacheslav Ivanov, Andrej Bely or Valery

◀ Boris Pasternak and his brother Alexander (*c.* 1905)

Gorky

Chekhov

Bryusov were unable to exercise a direct influence upon literary development in Western Europe—the difficulties of translation stood in their way—but it is sufficient to remind oneself of the Russian artists of that time who worked in media which had no need of translation, Scriabin and Stravinsky, Kandinsky and the forces which Diaghilev brought together in his ballet. They, and many others, testify to the strength and importance of the new discoveries which the poets of their country were also making at this time. The talents and moods of the Symbolists ranged from aestheticism to metaphysical mysticism, from neo-classicism to a dedication to mankind, with a willingness to suffer in this cause. Two of these artists, Blok and Bely, exercised the strongest influence on Boris Pasternak. Blok was, as a poet, undoubtedly the greater of the two. The power and beauty of his images, his deep humanity and sincere approach, left a lasting impression on Pasternak's work. Bely, on the other hand, was the most brilliant and fascinating personality in the ranks of the Symbolists. Torn between anthroposophic dreams and the orderliness of mathematical formulae—he was influenced by Rudolf Steiner and Albert Einstein both in his thought and in his writing—his style acquired a strong rhythm and he resorted to unusual words and images. Both poets were fired by a like revolutionary ardour, which turned against the ossified world of the Tsarist regime and the stifling bourgeois atmosphere—but which differed in conception and spirit from the forces that brought about the Revolution, and into whose camp they were later to drift for a while.

The year 1905 saw the first Russian revolution,
which was crushed with great loss
of life. Police and Cossack regiments
attacked the rebels

The monk, Georgy Gapon, led
the protesting, unarmed crowd to
the Winter Palace in St Petersburg and
to the Police Headquarters. The
streets were littered with the dead

While the intellectual revolt of the poets was manifesting itself in the written word, the
social forces which eventually broke up the old order became increasingly articulate. The
year 1905 saw the outbreak of the first Russian revolution, an eruption of natural forces
without plan or clearly defined aim. The Russo-Japanese war was lost to the Tsar; the
conditions of the peasants and workers were becoming more and more wretched; a rebellious
atmosphere was spreading. It was not actually directed against the person of the Tsar, but
rather against the machinery of suppression. On January 9, 1905, a huge crowd collected
in front of the Winter Palace in St Petersburg to complain to the Sovereign of their misery.
Georgy Gapon, the prison chaplain, led the crowd, but the strikes which had begun a
few days previously in the Putilov works in St Petersburg had made the police jumpy.
The authorities thought it advisable to teach the demonstrators a lesson. There were more
than three thousand dead and wounded among the unarmed crowd on this 'Bloody Sunday' after Cossacks and other army units had driven them back from the Winter Palace.
But this was only the beginning of the revolutionary crisis. In many towns general strikes
broke out, barricades were built and street fighting flared up. In Moscow the forces of
the Revolution concentrated in the district of Presnja. The workers' militia took up their
positions behind road blocks; there were exchanges of fire and short artillery bombard-
ments: and all the time demonstrators paraded the streets, ever on the look-out for the
cavalry units whose business it was to disperse the crowds. It is certain that Boris Pasternak,

now fifteen years old, could not have escaped the general excitement. He recalls the memories of those days in the opening chapters of his *Dr Zhivago*, and the atmosphere is very vividly evoked by his description of the column of demonstrators who take refuge in a school from the threat of Cossack attacks. What Boris Pasternak must have felt in those days when, during one of the demonstrations, he received a blow from a nagaika (the Cossack whip) was probably not so much the anger of the revolutionary as indignation at the harshness and inhumanity with which the demonstrators were treated.

In any case he did not join any of the social revolutionary or reformist groups of the Russian intelligentsia. For him, for his family, for their friends, life went on almost unchanged. Even his meeting with Maxim Gorky, who negotiated with Leonid Pasternak about contributions to politico-satirical newspapers, made no difference. Much more important to his development was the long journey which took the Pasternaks for six months to Berlin. This was the first long trip abroad for Boris. Berlin was full of Russian artists, philosophers and students, who had gone there to escape Tsarist censorship, but the young man was impressed by the town itself more than by its intellectual society. He wrote, 'I settled down quickly in Berlin, went for walks through its endless streets, spoke German with an imitation Berlin accent, breathed a mixture of the smoke of the steam engines, the smell of the gas lamps and beer froth, and I listened to Wagner.'

In the meantime a veritable artistic fever had broken out in Russia. Groups of painters of the most modern schools vied with each other, united, organized exhibitions. French art made its entry with Bonnard and Vuillard, Rodin and Matisse. Publishing houses and literary periodicals sprang up like mushrooms. In literary circles young art enthusiasts fought out their feuds. The Futurists burst upon the scene, declaring war against all the conventions of the bourgeois world, indeed, against all previous artistic values. A few years later they were to publish their manifesto under a title which was so typical of those years— 'A Slap in the Face for Public Taste'. But restlessness among the younger intellectuals was growing and could not be ignored. In literary circles new theories of art were being hatched. There were heated nocturnal discussions on poetry and philosophy, and, for reasons incomprehensible to the older generation, the young people went for long midnight walks. Here, again, it is difficult to fit Boris Pasternak into any particular group. He was still searching for the path he should take: as yet he could not even choose between music and literature. His friends, who drew him into a literary coterie called Serdarda, respected him for his musical talent—his vivacious and passionate improvisations on the piano. These people were attracted to a circle which had formed around the romantic and symbolistic periodical 'Musaget', which was closely connected with the neo-Kantian thinking of German philosophy. Meanwhile Pasternak was studying at Moscow University. He chose a subject which his father had chosen before him, in order to acquire a cer-

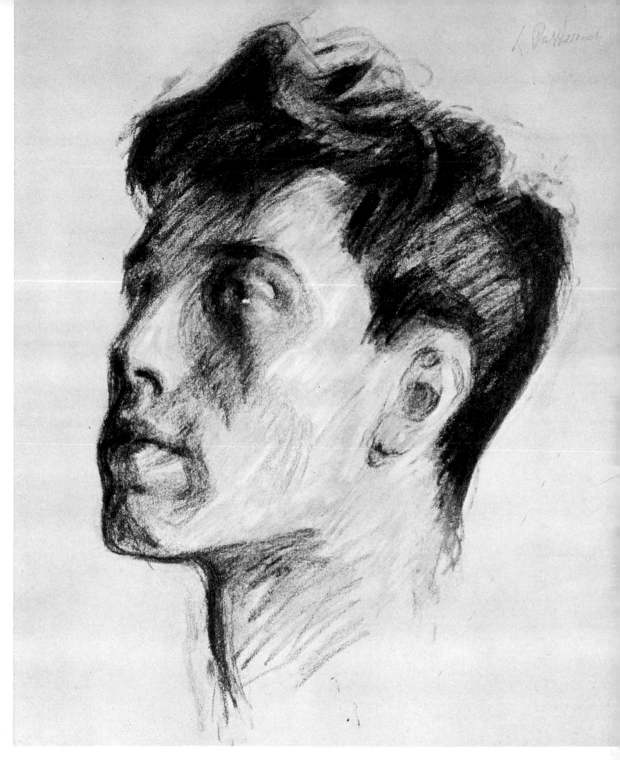

Boris Pasternak as a student. (Drawing by Leonid Pasternak)

tain academic basis of practical value. For simplicity's sake, as Boris Pasternak himself has put it, the faculty of Law was the one which he decided to embrace. But he did not remain faithful to it for long. On the advice of Alexander Scriabin he changed over—not to music, which had already begun to take second place to literature, but to philosophy. In order to make himself materially independent, he coached scholars and prepared them for matriculation. Now and then he spent his evenings with other students in a furnished flat where adults from many professions allowed themselves to be introduced into the mysteries of intellectual life by the young academicians.

Few of the University lectures were able to satisfy him: much of what was taught was too dull and arid for this young man whose youthful enthusiasm demanded stronger meat. He did not think much of his own literary attempts at that time, and received his friends' encouraging criticisms with incredulity. His contribution to the circle of his friends con- sisted at first mainly of artistic theory. In a sculptor's studio Boris, now nineteen years old, arranged a debate on 'Symbolism and Immortality'. Here he tried to explain his theory of artistic immortality to an audience who were partly sitting on the floor and partly lying on a gallery, with their heads over the side.

In 1909 Boris Pasternak began to study Law at the old Moscow University

In 1910 Leo Tolstoy died. Leonid Pasternak, who went to the funeral with his son, drew him as he lay on his death-bed

It was on that very same evening that Boris, deeply stirred by his own oration and the subsequent discussion, arrived home rather late to learn that Leo Tolstoy had met a lonely death on the railway station of Astapovo. A telegram summoned Leonid Pasternak to Yasnaya Polyana. Boris went with his father and saw in Astapovo the enormous crowd, drawn from people in every walk of life, who came to pay homage to the great man when his body was taken by students back to the home whence he had fled. Leo Tolstoy whose spirit, according to the Pasternak children, had pervaded their whole house, was dead. Tolstoy left as a heritage to his friend Leonid Pasternak a message which his son was to remember: 'You must realize, Leonid Ossipovich, that all will pass: money, large estates, even kingdoms are doomed to vanish, but if there is only one grain of true art in our work it will live for ever.'

Russian students were greatly attracted by the German universities of that time. The young philosopher no less than the young scientist, succumbed to the lure of their renown, and, indeed, the echo of their influence is still discernible among Soviet students. Boris Pasternak's intellectual friends were to be found among those lecturers and students of Moscow University who were adherents of the Marburg School of Philosophy, led by

the neo-Kantian Professor Cohen. Among the warring factions at Moscow University this group was the weakest, since it lacked professorial leadership. They had to defend themselves against the followers of Husserl and Bergson, who reigned supreme in the philosophical field at that time. But it was due to this struggle that philosophy did not remain empty speculation, but became a living faith. In April 1912 Rosa Pasternak made her eldest son a present of 200 roubles which she had saved from her housekeeping money and from music lessons given to particular gifted students at the Conservatoire, and there was never the slightest doubt as to the purpose to which he would put the money. His first outlay went to defray the cost of sending for the summer term curriculum at Marburg University. At that time there were hardly any obstacles in the way of a Russian who wanted to study abroad. Before the first World War passports, entry and exit visas and foreign exchange permits were only of minor importance. What was needed was money—yet, if one was very careful, not a great deal of it. Two hundred roubles were enough for the cheapest possible railway ticket, for lodgings and for food of the simplest kind. They enabled Boris Pasternak, then twenty years of age, to travel to Marburg, to stay there for one term, and to go from there to Italy.

That summer term at Marburg had a marked influence on Boris Pasternak's work. He was enchanted, and accepted the Marburg school of thought unreservedly, passionately, with avid enthusiasm. The reasons for such a response lay in the intrinsic character of that philosophy and in his own personality. What he learned in Marburg gave his own philosophy, the nucleus of which was already formed, a systematic framework without turning him wholly into a philosopher, or forcing him into the limited field of a school of philosophy. The Marburg school 'was independent: it rased everything to its foundations and rebuilt in free and wide open spaces. It had nothing in common with the sluggish routine of all the various "isms" that clung tenaciously to their profitable omniscience which they had gained at tenth hand—ever ignorant, and, for this or that reason, in permanent fear of exposing the centuries-old culture to the fresh air of new conceptions. Free from any terminological inertia, the Marburg school concerned itself with origins—that is to say, with the genuine traces of human thought in the history of science. While ordinary philosophy deals with the way of thinking of this or that author, and ordinary psychology explores the mental processes of men in general, while formal logic teaches us how to

Boris Pasternak's particulars as entered on the students' matriculation register at the University of Marburg

The University of Marburg, where Boris Pasternak spent the summer term of 1912

think in order to get the proper change in a baker's shop, the Marburg school was interested in the way scientific thought throughout twenty-five centuries had dwelt upon the
fiery beginning and upon the end of the world's discoveries. Such a conception which, as
it were, was lent authority by history itself, made philosophy unrecognizably young and
wise again, and changed it from a problematic study to the age-old study of problems,
which is what it should have been from the beginning.'

Hermann Cohen

Nikolai Hartmann

In his book *Safe Conduct* Pasternak has described in great detail his feelings during his Marburg days—his little room in an outer suburb, his old landlady (the widow of an official), the small university town, lectures by Hartmann and Professor Cohen. He speaks of a romantic entanglement, the result of the unexpected visit to Marburg of an early love. Already as an adolescent he had adored her. In the trying months before his matriculation he had given her private lessons in order to be with her. The continual presence of a French governess, however, had made it impossible for the eighteen-year-old Boris to tell her of his feelings towards her. His love for this pretty girl from a good family had been known to all his friends—or had been suspected by them—but Boris had never spoken to her of his love. Now she herself had come with her sister to Marburg on their way from Belgium to Berlin. When he writes of her he only gives the initial 'W'. Their three days together in a strange town, their long walks and talks together, ended in crisis. A few minutes before she was due to depart he declared his love, but she refused him! At the station, still suffering from the after-effect of this shock, he made the conventional farewells, but, as the train started to move, Boris ran alongside and at the very last moment jumped on to the footboard of her carriage. After the guard had been placated, the train carried him and the girl to Berlin together. But her mind was already made up, and what they had to say to

The narrow streets and the houses with their timber framework in the old part of Marburg fascinated the young Russian student. He lived in the house in the Gysselbergstrasse (left) which, in *Safe Conduct*, he called Giessener Street

each other now were only ghostly echoes of those hours spent together before his beloved had rejected him. Their farewells in Berlin were merely a parting of the ways, and the despondent suitor wandered through the gentle Berlin rain without a hat, without an overcoat, without money; finally, placing his head on a wooden table-top in a pub, he fell asleep.

This experience brought on the crisis which had been threatening for some time. The young student from Moscow was not to become a scientist or a philosopher. He returned to Marburg, to his landlady who had received her lodger's absence with shocked surprise, and collected up the books and papers which were strewn around his room in carefully planned disorder, and sent them back to the University library. He no longer worked on his thesis, but wrote verses instead. 'On every occasion, day and night, I wrote poems about the sea, the twilight, the southern rain, the coal of the Harz district. I wrote, immersed in my task, and a different kind of dust now covered my table. The previous dust, the philo-sophic one, had come from my disloyalty, my anxiety over my work. The new dust I left undisturbed out of a feeling of fellowship with, and sympathy for, the paving-stones in the Giessener Street. And at the far end of the oil-cloth covering my table a tumbler, long unwashed, glittered like a star in the sky.'

After this summer term in Marburg he went to Italy. The journey was made in a fourth-class carriage; he economized in food and lodgings. The ageing Boris Pasternak writes of this youthful journey, 'In the grey dawn I stumbled out of the train—I travelled through the night to save the money for an hotel—and often I was not sure whether I was walking around Milan Cathedral, or whether I was already in Florence.' But over and above the memories of lightly-borne privations on these voyages of discovery, crowd others—memories of the impact that classical Italian art made upon the young Russian. This art, with its countless documents from the centuries of man's past, was to him a clear demonstration of the eternal flow of culture—ever in motion, and yet calm within itself, changing without disrupting. To an Italian this may be the ordinary heady air which he breathes every day; to a young man from Russia this manifestation of ages of human culture, full of life and form, was a startling discovery.

And this young man who returned to Moscow was a poet. His outward appearance alone impressed his friends, and even strangers. The Russian painter Annenkhov gives this description of Boris Pasternak before the first World War, 'He had large eyes, full lips, a proud and dreamy bearing, a good figure, a rhythmic way of walking and a strong, pleasant voice. People in the street turned instinctively to look at him without knowing who he was. I remember how Pasternak himself once stopped, turned round, and, planting himself firmly on both feet, put his tongue out at a girl who had stared at him. "Now, look here——" I reproached him. "I am so shy, and curiosity embarrasses me," Pasternak replied apolo-getically.'

His parents did not show a great deal of understanding for his writing. With an indul-gent smile they let him do as he pleased, particularly since he showed no signs of poetic frenzy, but continued his philosophical studies, and passed his finals. In the following summer months he wrote the poems of his first book, *The Twin in the Clouds*. It made him the subject of literary discussions.

The various literary circles carried on feuds, formed splinter groups, and behaved as if each alone were in possession of the only new truth. All this, no doubt, served to justify their existence. But Boris Pasternak did not seem to fit into any one of these groups. In

In 1912 Pasternak left Marburg for Italy. Milan Cathedral (above) and the buildings of Venice and Florence made a deep impression upon him

the end he was counted among 'the right wing of Futurism', a moderate group, which took no really active part in the efforts that were being made to condemn all traditional art as senseless and outdated. Partisanship was contrary to his nature, and more especially he did not wish to take sides against the great poetry of the Symbolists which had had such a strong influence on his first volume of poems.

Moscow 1914—on the surface an idyll fit
for a museum. Already undermined, however,
only three years of tranquillity remained to it

However, he joined the group of writers called 'Centrifuge', and had to fight in its
cause. Over cake and hot milk in a cafe in Arbat Square, he used to wait with his friends
for 'the enemy'. The leader of their three antagonists was a tall conspicuous man with
strong features and a sonorous voice, who was destined to become a beacon among the
noisy crowd of second-raters and fellow-travellers in the hyper-individualistic battle against
all artistic convention; later, as the 'mouthpiece of the Revolution', he was to dominate
the first ten years of Soviet literature. His name was Mayakovsky.

Vladimir Mayakovsky was three years younger than Boris Pasternak, but in the Futurist
movement his pale-yellow jacket had already become the symbol for bourgeois fears. He
was expelled from school for having joined the Bolshevist wing of the Russian Social
Democrats, but later he showed considerable talent as a student at the Moscow School of
Painting, Sculpture and Architecture. Although he was not yet twenty, he was among
the most conspicuous of the Futurists—not only because of his yellow jacket and his anti-
bourgeois activities, but because he was the poetic genius of the group. Yet by 1914 he
seems to have long given up his preoccupation with the social themes that had interested
him in his youth. He mocked the poets who acted as 'Prophets of truth and advertisements

30

of virtue'. His declaration of faith in purely formalist art sounded a little hollow, and, however loudly he repeated it, his own poems belied him. In spite of all his experiments with metre, all his distortions of syntax, all his over-elaborated inventions of new words, he did not present the reader with works of formalist art but with speeches—rhetorical, declamatory, full of pathos. When the tall Mayakovsky delivered them in his loud voice, the strong rhythm of the verses made even the consciously anti-poetical poetic.

When he compared the stars in heaven with drops of spittle, and himself with a hot pavement upon which a woman throws kisses in the shape of cigarette butts—he was not out to shock the bourgeoisie, but being true to the poet in him.

Pasternak was to meet Mayakovsky in his capacity of the man who had insulted the 'Centrifuge' in the course of a literary squabble, but he was no longer interested in petty quarrels among the factions. He recognized in Mayakovsky a colossus standing apart from the noisy crowd of second-raters. 'Behind the surface one felt something like a decision come to fulfilment, the consequences of which were irrevocable. His genius was such a decision; and having once become aware of it, he was so deeply impressed that it became the guiding theme for him to follow for ever. . . . .' During the ensuing years Mayakovsky,

Boris Pasternak (left) and Vladimir
Mayakovsky met before the first World War
as literary foes. Soon
they became friends

whose yellow jacket always served as a symbol of outward independence, remained for
Boris the much-admired and loved, albeit distant, friend—until such time as he discarded
his symbol and became the booming political poet of the first post-revolutionary years;
though, in the long run, this activity could not quell the restlessness within him.

In August 1914 the first World War broke out. The great catastrophe had begun.
The pathos of the war stimulated some of the young and some of the older poets, and at
first Mayakovsky could not escape it. But neither he nor his friend, though they both volun-
teered for the forces, were destined to wear military uniform. The injury to his knee which
he had incurred when he fell from the horse made Pasternak unfit for military service.
During the first anti-German riots he saw the house of a German merchant go up in flames.
This was a house in which he had worked for some time as a tutor to the merchant's son,
Walter Philipp; in the building, which the crowd methodically destroyed, some of his
personal belongings and manuscripts were burned to ashes. By that time he had already
taken another job as a tutor—to the sons of the poet Baltrushaitis on his estate on the river
Oka. In addition, he had started his first longer translation; it was Heinrich von Kleist's
play *Der Zerbrochene Krug*, to be performed in the Moscow Kamerny Theatre. During this

Caricature of Mayakovsky, the
'Revolutionary Drummer'

time he also wrote the poems of his second book, *Above the Barriers*, and he prepared his
first work in prose (the most important piece of early prose), *The Childhood of Luvers*, which
he finished later in the chaotic year of the Civil War of 1918.

But the world of painters and poets in that peaceful estate on the Oka did not hold
Pasternak for long. After travelling through many parts of Russia he reached a little town
in the Urals. There, in the chemical works of Uchkov, which were of great importance
to the Russian war effort, Pasternak worked in the management. He was the head of the
military department of the works, and it was his job to make sure that in spite of the call-
up, a sufficient number of workers remained in the factory to keep up production. The
only connection which this small town had with the war was the factory. In the winter
the outside world seemed to be blotted out by a white curtain of snow; and the first reports
of the February Revolution in Petrograd came to the little town in the Urals as if from
far off. But the news was exciting enough. In March, Boris Pasternak stepped into a troika
(a sledge drawn by three horses) which carried the mail, and left the peaceful snow-clad
countryside to make his way to Moscow.

The unrest began with hunger marches and strikes; it culminated in a general strike,

Alexander III

The empire of the Tsars in which Boris
Pasternak grew up came to an abrupt end in 1917.
Tsar Nicholas II was deposed, kept a prisoner
and later murdered. In the parliament in
Petrograd, the 'Duma (right), sat the Workers'
and Soldiers' Councils

Nicholas II

whereupon the garrisons refused to shoot at the rebel workers. The Revolution had come! The foundations of the administration, the army, the police, the merchants and landed gentry—all those pillars which in 1905 had still supported the autocracy—had crumbled in the war years. They had lost faith in the Tsar. It needed only a gentle push to make the whole edifice tumble. The forces which had prepared the end of the retrogressive feudal world stood disconcerted and without a plan in face of this sudden collapse. Neither the upper middle-classes, which should have formed a provisional government, nor the workers, whose aims found expression in the 'Soviets', were ready for such an abrupt fall of the Tsarist regime—and least of all, perhaps, the Communists, whose leader, Lenin,

In the spring of 1917 there were repeated demonstrations in the streets of Petrograd and Moscow

had stated only a few weeks previously in far-away Switzerland that he did not know whether he would see the Revolution in his lifetime.

The majority of the Russian intelligentsia welcomed the February Revolution as the great new prelude which had smashed the musty bourgeois world and the dusty Tsarist apparatus, so that man's new freedom could be built upon the debris of the past. For them it was not the social and political changes that were of primary importance but the collapse of an intellectual world against which they had already been fighting for years. Alexander Blok came out on the side of the revolutionaries. Andrei Bely returned from Switzerland. The Futurists saw in this world of confusion and destruction the proof of

The head of the revolutionary government, Kerensky (centre), makes a desperate fight against the Bolsheviks

In October 1917 Kerensky's followers were massacred in the streets of Petrograd

their theory which rejected all conventional values in art. They saw themselves as the poets of the Revolution, and they did everything in their power to be acknowledged as the spiritual executors of its mood and trends.

In this half-year of disorder, which did not allow enough time for the opposing forces to strike a new balance, the conflict between the literary groups grew. Boris Pasternak, whom his friends regarded as belonging to the 'revolutionary poetical forces', found himself in a different wing of the Futurists from Mayakovsky. There was tension and there were quarrels; these did not, however, affect their admiration and respect for each other's art. But Pasternak had changed since his early contacts with the Futurists. This romantic extrovert literary movement did not satisfy him any longer. His second volume of poems, *Above the Barriers*, which was published in that year, already showed an estrangement from an art which, in its fight against the philistines, was in danger of exhausting itself with

The storming of the Winter Palace. The Reds take charge of the Revolution

no more than a threatening gesture against the middle classes. The splendid cloak of the poetic orator was not to be his. He was incapable of making dramatic, romantic, self-important overstatements. He gave up this pose before it acquired heroic proportions and the odour of blood, and he tried to limit himself to the actual craft of verse-making. Yet he did not lose his way in experiments with form. He neither let himself be seduced by the events of the moment into writing topical biased poetry, nor did he try to build an ivory tower of pure art divorced from life. He tried to give expression to everything in man that is greater than man himself. He searched amid the revolutionary turmoil, which he regarded as a great natural catastrophe, for the clear features of an ethical and moral humanity, and for the simple laws governing life and experience. When told that in such times it was of paramount importance to react quickly and to shoot quickly, he answered only, 'In an epoch of speed one must think slowly.'

Pasternak did not regard the assumption of power by the Communists in October 1917 as a catastrophe; nor did he see it as the victory of the most modern political system in the world. He neither emigrated, as so many Russian writers did in the years following, nor did he join others in penning intoxicated eulogies to machines and factories. His mind worked slowly. That year he wrote a work in prose which had nothing whatever to do with war or revolution. It is a story that has no real plot, a tale of a girl who has just crossed the threshold of puberty, built up from innumerable careful observations, without definite beginning or end. This is a piece of prose which is unique in Russian literature. In method the story is related to the works of Proust. Of *The Childhood of Luvers*, and indeed of all Pasternak's early prose, could be said what Ortega y Gasset said of Marcel Proust, 'Proust's characters are without outline: they are unsubstantial wraiths, intellectual images which change constantly in a breath of air or a ray of light. Proust is undoubtedly "the explorer" of the human soul in the Stendhal tradition.' The detailed description of environment, the psychological observation of emotions, is in Pasternak's case never verbose or over-protracted. On the contrary, in the concentrated intensity of his style each word is laden with deep meaning—almost overladen, in fact. This tightly packed method of presentation demands almost too much from the reader. There are no points at which he can relax and digest what he has read; there are no links, no explanations. Pasternak tries to produce in the reader a certain definite sensation, and he omits everything that he considers superfluous to the achievement of this aim. But in spite of all these difficulties, and its strange and unusual style, *The Childhood of Luvers* was to remain, in its pure translucence and gentle charm, his most beautiful and important early work in prose. When this story appeared seven years later in a volume of Pasternak's prose, the critics praised it as one of the most important pieces of prose of the first period of Soviet art.

In an earlier short novel called *Il Tratto di Apelle*, Pasternak had explored the possibilities of poetic irony in his description of the romantic adventures of the young Heine in Italy. 'In one single line', he says there, 'I must express all my being, all that is vital in my art.' He then goes on to say, 'This is the simplest, and therefore the most difficult thing that one can attain.' Even in this rather ill-balanced novel one can already recognize the typical features of Pasternak's art.

In 1918 a second short work of prose was produced, *Letters from Tula*. It is written in a high-flown expressionistic style, and falls below the standard of Pasternak's best writing. In it one can see sure traces of the Revolution, the Civil War, and the new regime, and one feels that it is a protest against the cliché-ridden art of those who, by acclaiming the new era, tried to make things easy for themselves. It is a challenge to conscience—a poet examining himself. 'The poet—from now on we shall put this word in inverted commas until he is cleansed by fire—the "poet" sees his own image in the unseemly behaviour

Pasternak's mother and his sisters
at the piano. (Drawing by Leonid Pasternak, 1917)

1921 Москва
В ВЦИК говорит ... Плен
В.Ц.И.К.

of the actors and in the outrageous drama which points the finger of accusation at his comrades and his generation.' Then it was that the 'poet' realized that he was in Tula, a place closely associated with the name of Tolstoy. 'No wonder if the needle of the compass begins to dance here. Everything that happens here stems from the essence of this place. This is an event in the realm of conscience.'

The man who wrote this could not take part in squabbles about literary trends. The Futurists denounced the Symbolists to the revolutionary authorities as the relics of bourgeois thought. The Cosmists sang in pompous romantic tones the praises of machines, factories, life in the Collectives. Others called for the destruction of the museums. The adherents of the 'cult of the proletariat' maintained that only former workers and soldiers were suitable to be the poets of modern times. Every group sought recognition by the Communists as the only legitimate representatives of revolutionary art. With art involved in this political chase, poetry itself was in danger of suffocation. Poets starved, as did that experimenting Futurist, the vagabond, Velemir Khlebnikov; they were shot as counter-

The new masters of Russia:
Lenin and, behind him,
seated, Stalin and Kalinin. (Drawing
by Leonid Pasternak, 1921)

Boris Pasternak took no part
in the Revolution. At that time
his poetry had no political content.
Although many Russian intellectuals emigrated at the beginning of
the 'twenties, he remained in
Russia. (Photo c. 1920)

revolutionaries, like Nikolai Gumilev, whom Maxim Gorky tried in vain to save; they died from want and disillusionment, like Alexander Blok. This poet, so dearly loved by Pasternak, was enthusiastic in his praise of the October Revolution of the Bolsheviks. In 1921, six months before he died, he lamented the loss of creative freedom. 'The poet dies for lack of air. Life has lost its meaning.'

Vladimir Mayakovsky and Sergei Yesenin, the most renowned poets of those years, still allowed themselves to be carried on the wave of revolutionary pathos. Yesenin, who was called the peasant poet because of his dazzling earthy images (but he was much greater than such a label could ever suggest) had gathered around him the Imaginists, who, in their crazy exuberance, far surpassed the Futurists. He described with vicious and blas

Maxim Gorky was particularly
close to the Red Revolutionaries.
When, in 1921, they intervened
in the literary field, he so
often rallied to the defence
of writers who were threatened,
that it was suggested to him that
he should leave Russia for
a time. He departed,
in a spirit of resignation

Alexander Blok, an early victim
of disillusionment about the
Revolution: 'The poet dies
because he cannot breathe
any longer'

phemous images the peasant paradise which was to come—departing further and further
from the moving and profound descriptions of Russian nature, while he let himself be
drawn ever faster into wild, wanton living. Disillusioned and desperate he sought refuge
in a journey round the world and in a brief marriage with Isadora Duncan. Vladimir
Mayakovsky, on the other hand, tried to subordinate his own nature to the requirements
of everyday politics. He made himself the 'drummer' and 'mouthpiece' of the Revolution,
and started to pen pompous poems to the glory of the new regime. He claimed that he
despised poetry and insisted that it was not in keeping with the times. In a different way
from that of Yesenin, but for the same reason, he tried to give his life meaning and stability
by assuming the romantic pose of the revolutionary.

Sergei Yesenin

In the meantime Boris Pasternak had taken a post as a librarian. And he wrote poems which were to bring him recognition as the most important lyrical author among the post-revolutionary generation of writers. But he did not live in an ivory tower, even though he rarely commented on the problems of the day. In 1922 he published, in the periodical *Sovremennik,* an article with the title *A Few Observations on Art.* This contains a sentence which bears testimony to his character and to his work, 'We have forgotten that there is only one thing in our power: not to distort the living voice of life.' He took no part in the quarrels of the men of letters, but at the same time he did not seek to evade the challenge to bear witness to his own nature. He writes:

Vladimir Mayakovsky

I am ashamed
Daily I am more ashamed
That in an era of such shadows
A certain serious malady
Is called song.
Hell is paved with good intentions.
They say, if your verses
Are paved with them too
All your sins will be forgiven.
This pains the ear of silence. . . .

Yesenin dreamed too vividly
of the State of the future
to be able to bear the present.
Nor did he find help in
his brief marriage to
Isadora Duncan (here seen
in a motorcar with him). In 1925
he committed suicide

In 1922 his volume of poems *My Sister, Life* was published in Berlin. In those days there was nothing unusual in this. Many Russian publishing firms which had sprung up as private enterprises in the era of the 'new economic policy' had their printing done abroad. The inflation in Germany made Berlin a very suitable place, and, apart from that, there were many Russian writers in Berlin—emigrants and people who had not yet made up their minds, and who were to return to Russia later. Maxim Gorky too was there, for he had been sent from the Soviet Union for a period of convalescence, in order that he, who was always ready to champion writers against the Party, should not himself turn away in bitterness from the Party. **Boris's** parents had been resident in Berlin for the past year. Rosa Pasternak had suffered severely from heart trouble during the period of war and revolution, and in those turbulent and bitter years it was unlikely that she would be able to get quick medical attention in the Soviet Union. Leonid Pasternak therefore left for Germany, where his wife had already been treated before the war. Both daughters, Josephine and Lydia, accompanied their parents: the sons, Boris and Alexander, remained in the Soviet Union. The Pasternak family had not emigrated. They kept their Soviet citizenship

In 1921 Boris Pasternak's parents left Russi
Leonid Pasternak set up his stud
in Berlin (where he is shown, right, with h
wife in front of his easel). Left: the poe
mother. (Drawing by Leonid Pasterna

Sketches by Leonid Pasternak from his
Berlin years
Gustav Stresemann (right) and Albert Einstein,
playing the violin (below)

Lovis Corinth was one of Pasternak's clo
friends. They often sat for e
other. A portrait of Pasternak pai
by Corinth in 1923 hangs in
Hamburg Kunsth

'The soul parts with the West': it is the destiny of Russian intellectuals to long for Europe and for brotherhood with the West. This longing possessed Pushkin (right), Dostoyevsky (left)—and Pasternak

and, right up to the day of his death in London in 1945, Leonid kept a portrait of Lenin on his easel. In Berlin he lived as a well-known and respected portrait painter, and Corinth and Liebermann, Hauptmann and Einstein sat for him. In 1922, the year in which the volume of poems *My Sister, Life* appeared in Berlin, Boris visited Germany. With his future wife, Evgenya, who was a painter, he once more visited the old town of Marburg. In Berlin he took some part in literary discussions among the Russian intellectuals, but then he returned to Moscow. Berlin was not his world.

> *With the undried tears of parting,*
> *Having wept through the night,*
> *The soul takes leave of the West,*
> *Where it can never belong . . .*

But the West, which was not his world, did not loosen its grip on Boris Pasternak. His encounter with West European culture, with the spirit of the poetry of the West, had made too deep an imprint on him to make it possible for him to wrench himself completely free. The fact that he had a strong affinity with the spiritual heritage of Russia as well as with that of Western Europe was an advantage for the poet which few Russian writers

are vouchsafed; at the same time it was a burden for a man living in the Soviet Union—a country which isolated itself more and more from Europe, which turned its face to the Urals, and which transferred its capital from the cosmopolitan city of Petrograd to Moscow, in the interior. The words which Dostoyevsky wrote in praise of Pushkin could also in truth be said of Pasternak. 'He possessed in his soul the genius of many lands, and he revealed in his creative efforts the universality of the struggle of the Russian spirit. Had he lived longer he could, by the force of his genius, have made the Russian soul immortal, he could have brought it nearer to our European family, and made it simpler to under-stand.' But Russia had renounced the European family, and what for the dead Pushkin would have been praise, if said about the living Pasternak would have been a deadly insult.

Nevertheless, in those years when literary life was relatively free, Pasternak won almost unlimited praise and recognition. His new volume of poems, *Themes and Variations*, appeared in 1924 (the year in which his first son, Evgeny, was born) and with it he established his position among the young Russian poets. In spite of the fact that he avoided romantic pathos and declamatory gestures, he took his place next to Yesenin and Mayakovsky. They were the three brilliant stars of those years—but one of those stars was already setting.

In 1925, in the Hotel Astoria in Leningrad, Sergei Yesenin cut his arteries, wrote a farewell letter in his own blood, and hanged himself.

Mayakovsky once again paraded as the practical revolutionary who did not think such a romantic death befitted the times. 'Have you lost your reason, Yesenin? Is there not in the world enough ink to write a farewell letter? Why increase the number of suicides? It is much better to increase ink production', and he answered Yesenin's farewell with:

> *To die is here on earth no art.*
> *The harder task is building life.*

In his disillusionment with the Revolution and swept along in the maelstrom of an hysterically exaggerated *joie de vivre*, Yesenin could not find his way back to the source which had given his poetry strength. Mayakovsky for his part took refuge in political action. As the 'mouthpiece' of the Revolution he declared that he wished to crush the 'throat of his own singing'. His yellow jacket, the erstwhile symbol of his independence, was replaced by this new pose as the revolutionary people's poet. Pasternak, who many

In 1925 the new rulers in the Kremlin imposed final control over literature. Stalin gave his directives, Bukharin (seen right, next to Stalin), the ideologist of the Party, formulated them. Mayakovsky immediately toed the line, Yesenin committed suicide, Pasternak, stood aloof. And Gorky waited in Italy (left) . . .

years before had repudiated the romantic attitude as a way of living, kept his objective point of view towards himself and the events in the world around him. He tried, with the 'craft of poetic art', and within the limits of his own capability, to come to terms with the experiences and events of his world.

The year 1925 was a turning-point in the history of Soviet literature. The Central Com-mittee of the Communist Party issued a 'literary manifesto'. Many writers considered it to be the Magna Carta of their freedom, and, indeed, it did put a curb on the extremists who championed the so-called proletarian art to the exclusion of all else. The 'literary experts' were buttressed, but, at the same time, the manifesto reaffirmed the fundamental principle that the Party must guide the development of art and literature. Twenty years earlier Lenin had already demanded partisanship from writers, but, for the time being, the Party concentrated on the liberal passages in Lenin's work. A small group of Soviet writers, including Pasternak, felt the 'literary manifesto' to be the first interference by the Party in the lives of men of letters. Most of the others, however, who had suffered under the extremist demands of the hegemony of the left-wing group of writers, were quite con-tent now that the Party seemed to favour a middle road.

58

After the death of Lenin (left)
a cold wind blew through
life in Russia.
It marked the beginning
of a new policy. The fight which Stalin
waged against his rival, Trotsky (right), as to
who should be
Lenin's successor,
threatened to split Russia into two camps

In those years the lyrical writers had lost their leading position in Soviet literature. This was not as a consequence of any order issued by the Party, but the almost forgotten art of novel writing appeared to have come into its own again, reborn from its own inherent strength. Fedin, Leonov and Sholokhov, to name only the most important among the young writers of prose, came to the fore with original, sincere and profound works. The general tendency to write in the epic form made itself felt in Pasternak's work, too. At the same time it became evident that for years he had been quietly trying to adjust himself to the Revolution, and to the State to which it had given birth. This found expression in the short story *Aerial Ways*, which he wrote in 1925. 'There are aerial ways in existence', he says in this work, which deals with the time before 1914 and the time of the Revolution, 'on which arrive daily, like trains, the direct thoughts of a Liebknecht, a Lenin and a few other intellects of equal stature. They were paths laid on a level plane, effective and strong enough to cross all frontiers, whatever their name. . . .' But the story ends with a mother losing her son in the turmoil of the Revolution which had released those direct thoughts.

Pasternak never succeeds in definitely identifying himself with the Communist revolution. Even his epic poem, *The Year 1905*, which deals with the first Russian revolution and the mutiny of the Black Sea fleet in a loosely connected sequence of lyrical impressions, got wrecked on the rocks of his own personality. Lieutenant Schmidt, who took sides with the mutinying sailors of the battleship *Potemkin*, does not represent in this epic what one really ought to understand as a conscious revolutionary. His protest remains lyrical and universally human. Pasternak's attempt to look for inspiration in social and political events, instead of, as previously, in nature and human experience, did not succeed.

But in those years the Party did not yet insist upon a declaration of its political credo. It did not demand that literature should be biased, and was content with the efforts of the 'fellow travellers', as long as they did not produce literature actually hostile to its policy. But Pasternak was no politician; this much his colleagues knew of him, even if he sometimes appeared to them as an enigma. A cartoonist once represented him as the Sphinx sitting beside a reading-lamp, surrounded by his friends. Even so, some of his utterances

Pasternak's epic poem *The Year 1905*
based on legends to which the Revolution gave rise. Events on the battleship
Potemkin (left), and the person
of Lieutenant Schmidt (right), who
in 1905 took the side of
the mutinying sailors of the
Black Sea fleet, play a symbolic role
in it. In 1917 this naval lieutenant was
already so much of a legendary figure that
the soldiers of the Red
Army in Leningrad named
one of their primitive tanks after him (below)

In 1928 Gorky returned to the Soviet Union.
He was needed and, therefore,
had to be tolerated. In front of Moscow railway
station, where Bukharin and
Khalatov (on Gorky's right) received
him, he was given a great ovation

'The Sphinx'—a caricature of
Boris Pasternak (c. 1925)

were distinctly heretical: 'Instead of speaking of this epoch in general, which indeed, is the task of the future, we have forced the epoch itself to be generalization personified.' But at that time the critics were still allowed to praise him.

D. S. Mirsky, the 'Red Prince' who had emigrated to England but had returned to the Soviet Union, wrote, 'He is the only Russian prose writer of today who still keeps in mind that neglected thing—the human soul', and, he added, his *The Childhood of Luvers* would in time 'be recognized as a work of profound importance, and an inspiration to a new and as yet unborn school of prose in the far distant future'.

Vladimir Pozner wrote, 'One day, when a balance sheet of our time is drawn up, then *The Childhood of Luvers* will head the credits.'

In 1930, Ilya Ehrenburg placed *The Childhood of Luvers* amongst the ten most important works of Soviet prose. He even said, 'It was Pasternak who laid the true foundation of Soviet art, and this is the reason why his creative strength has caused such bitter controversy in the past, and still does today.'

Pasternak's influence on the younger poets was unusually strong. Nearly all prominent Soviet lyric writers have to some extent been moulded by him. In one of Eduard Bagritsky's poems he is part of the iron ration:

> *Matches and tobacco*
> *in my rucksack*
> *and Tichonov,*
> *Selvinski,*
> *Pasternak.*

But the time of the great, bitter controversies, of which Ilya Ehrenburg spoke, had hardly begun. True, there were many who criticized Pasternak for the great difficulty they had in understanding his poems, and the fact that they had no connection with social reality. Vladimir Mayakovsky, although he was eager to disown his own lyrical writings, was enough of a poet to praise precisely those works by Pasternak which are not concerned

63

with the social and political realities—*Above the Barriers* and *My Sister, Life*. On the other hand, he did not think much of *The Year 1905*. It was he who invented the label which from then on was to cling to Pasternak—either by way of praise or of criticism—namely, a 'Poet's Poet'. This was actually the highest praise, but at the same time open to suspicion —in a time of literary mass consumption.

Vladimir Mayakovsky, having tried his hand at satirical plays, returned to lyric poetry. But he was disillusioned by the outcome of the Revolution. 'I am being accused of so many things, charged with so many sins, that, sometimes, I feel like going away somewhere for a few years so as not to have to listen any longer to abuse.' On April 14, 1930, he shot himself through the heart—this man, to whom five years previously, Yesenin's suicide had appeared as a romantic indiscretion.

'Well, there it is. We are different,' he had once told Pasternak. 'You like the lightning in the sky, and I like it in the electric circuit.' Pasternak, now the only survivor of the 'triad', was deeply shocked by the death of his estranged friend. Twenty-five years later,

1893 - 1930

Владимир Владимирович
Маяковский

Following Yesenin, Mayakovsky committed suicide in 1930. The literary revolutionaries had been destroyed by revolutionary reality. Of the 'three stars' of the 'twenties only the unpolitical Pasternak remained alive. Stalin (right) who favoured 'socialist realism' left the memory of the dead poet untouched. There were even postcards on sale with Mayakovsky's picture on them (left)

when remembering the suicides of his former comrades—of Yesenin and Mayakovsky, of Maria Tsvetayeva, Paolo Yashvili and Aleksei Fadeyev—he was to write of their deaths:

'When one contemplates suicide one obliterates oneself, one turns away from one's own past, one proclaims one's own bankruptcy, and one's memories are worthless. These memories can no longer touch one, to give succour or support. The continuity of one's inner existence is broken, the personality is dead. One does not kill oneself out of loyalty to a decision one has once taken, but because one is unable to bear that fear of unknown origin, that suffering which is not a physical suffering, this senseless waiting to which there is no fulfilment in continued life. . . . But they all suffered indescribably, they suffered to a degree where the feeling of fear had grown to lunacy. Let us bow our heads in pity for their suffering, as well as to their genius and their radiant memory.'

But this was written a quarter of a century later, after Pasternak had suffered years of fear during which he himself may have had reason enough to think of suicide. In 1930, at Mayakovsky's death-bed, he was forcefully reminded that 'This man may have been a

citizen of this country beyond compare. . . . He was spoiled from childhood by the future, which he mastered relatively early and without difficulty,' and he said modestly, 'To Mayakovsky was given the greatest destiny as a poet. Whenever our generation later expressed itself dramatically and lent a poet its voice, one heard in the ties which bound them together the echo of Mayakovsky's kindred note.'

Pasternak's difficulties during the years that followed were of a very ordinary and human kind. He himself does not give us any further information about this time. In his autobiographical essay, *Safe Conduct* (1931), he writes, 'Very soon after this there were in two families, in mine and in that of my friends, shocks, complications and changes, which were morally distressing for all who participated in them.' Pasternak obtained a divorce from his first wife, who then married the famous pianist Henrik Neyhaus. He himself travelled into the Caucasus with Zinaida Neyhaus, who later became his second wife. There Boris was to be the guest of the great Georgian poet, Paolo Yashvili, and having 'no place to lay his head', accepted the invitation. It was then that he got to know the Georgian poets, whose works he later translated into Russian. For a time he lived in Tiflis, and in his volume of poems, *Second Birth*, he writes of the view from his room on to the mountain-tops of the Caucasus, describing the oppressive beauty of these mountains as none has succeeded in doing since Lermontov.

After the volume *Second Birth*, which appeared one year after his autobiographical *Safe Conduct*, Pasternak published no more books for eleven years. In 1934 there appeared once more a 'provisional edition' of his collected poems, and once again the Great Soviet Encyclopaedia devoted a whole column to him:

'Boris Leonidovich Pasternak, born 1890, studied Philosophy in Moscow and Marburg. He tried to raise himself above the turmoil of the social struggle to the zenith of middle class culture, but all the time a quality of living vitality breaks through the bourgeois-idealist covering of his works. He, therefore, reflects the events of the fight for the dictatorship of the proletariat. . . . P. defends the freedom of his poetic creation in all circumstances and at all times. In the beginning he saw the Revolution as an elementary force of destruction. Finally he accepted it like a pathway to the sacrifice. The thesis of the poet on the incompatibility of art and socialism is bound up with the experience of a single fate, because to P. art is always the expression of the unique character of a single individual. For him socialism is only a cloud of smoke behind the fog of theories, and an epoch in which people "suspect" each other. It is a peculiarity of his lyrical work that he always gives two parallel aspects of a picture, and two parallel motives. His poetry is, as he himself says, a "hypnotic homeland". P's great genius has brought him a reputation as an original poet who exerts an influence on Soviet poetry.'

It was still possible to write this sort of thing in 1934, but when this volume of the Encyclopaedia was published Pasternak's day was already over; for, in this same year Stalin

Boris Pasternak.
A photograph taken in
the early 'thirties

proclaimed the doctrine of 'Socialist Realism'. And in the new literature there was no longer any room for Pasternak's work.

Since 1932 the swing of the pendulum had steadily become more pronounced. The various literary groups of the Soviet Union were amalgamated into the 'Association of Soviet Writers', and in August 1934 this new body organized its first national congress. Andrei Zhdanov, who was to dominate Soviet literature for the next twenty years, said, 'Yes, Soviet literature is indeed biased, because in an age of class warfare there cannot be, and there is not, a literature which stands above class.' All this belonged to the old tenets of the Party, but now that Stalin had promoted the writers to be 'engineers of the human soul', literature had to become the servant of the Party, or it would have ceased to exist. At this congress in 1934, however, there were still sharp controversies. The writers defended themselves, and Nikolai Bukharin (the 'darling of the Party', the man whom Lenin in his Testament called 'the most able of theorists') assumed the role of defender of modern

In 1936 Gorky, 'Stalin's friend', died. The circumstances of his death, for which the head of the OGPU, Yeshov, was held responsible, have still not been completely cleared up

literature. He condemned the unrelieved propaganda poetry of Mayakovsky's imitators: he defended the lyric, and declared that social realism had to take men into account, and ought not to produce poetry which was merely rhetoric, and lacked flesh and blood; and he praised Boris Pasternak as one of the 'most important masters of verse of our time'. This was the last time that Pasternak was praised in public. Four years later Bukharin was executed with the old guard of the Revolution as a 'spy of a hostile power'.

The Party's new line was to create a barrier between the Soviet reader and a large part of modern Russian and West European writing, and that barrier exists to this day. Joyce, Dos Passos, Proust were once more the subjects of heated discussions—only to be condemned. Soviet literature had from now on to be guided by the principles of style of the Russian realist writers at the turn of the century, and to produce works which entirely devoted themselves to 'the heroic fight of the world proletariat, and the inspiration of victorious socialism, which reflect the great wisdom and heroism of the Communist Party.'

The Party decides what literature is: Rykov, Rlynov, Bukharin, Rudzutak (from left to right). Soon they will be standing in the dock

Joyce   Dos Passos   Proust

The fact that, none-the-less, it was possible in the following years for books of permanent value to be written, books whose poetic content had not been destroyed by all the regimentation and changes, testifies to the astonishing miracle of the indestructible strength of Russian writing.

From then on Pasternak, who was always attacked and cited as a bad example, had no original work of his published until the time of the second World War. When he was the subject of a particularly sharp attack in the spring of 1936, D. S. Mirsky tried once more to defend him. Pasternak's poetry, he stated, played a greater role in the propagation of Soviet culture abroad, and in the conquest of Western intellectuals, than that of some of the representatives of 'Socialist Realism'. But this argument fell on deaf ears in the year 1936, just as it was to do twenty-two years later, when Boris Pasternak was awarded the Nobel Prize.

From the middle of the 'thirties onwards Pasternak published only translations. First and foremost he translated Shakespeare; his mastery in verse-making made him also a master of translation. This work was the source of his income, upon it rested his fame and his position in the Association of Soviet Writers. At the time of the great purges in which so many Soviet poets disappeared for ever, or were executed, no harm came to Pasternak, although he remained a controversial figure, and was unrelentingly critical. Nobody could explain how it was that he escaped the fate of so many of his friends; some thought that his translation of the Georgian poems was the reason for Stalin's benevolent forbearance.

In the middle 'thirties Western influence on Russian literature was condemned. Joyce, Dos Passos and Proust, previously respected as paragons, have become outlaws

Bukharin (right), whose protégé Pasternak was, was executed as a traitor in 1938

But these translations from Stalin's native tongue are no valid reason why Pasternak should have come through that time unharmed.

Before the beginning of the purges, Pasternak must already have been under immense stress, perhaps even subject to great fear. When, in 1935, he was sent to attend the Congress of Anti-Fascist Writers in Paris, he passed through Berlin. He had been loth to leave Russia. He was newly fitted out, he looked fit and well. But he was hardly prepared to exchange more than a few words of greeting with his sisters in Berlin. He retired into a darkened room and slept until his train was due to leave for Paris. He felt unable to talk about Russia with those old friends from pre-Revolutionary times whom he met there again. He wandered through the streets, and he visited the house in which Rilke had lived. It was not that he shirked his official obligations, but he withdrew into his own shell. Ilya Ehrenburg, who had also been sent to Paris, thought that Pasternak's behaviour was proof that he was absolutely egocentric, especially when he refused to have lunch with Cocteau and Malraux. He gave as an excuse that the early hour of the meal

Pasternak, while staying in Paris in 1935, fought shy of meeting André Malraux (lef and Jean Cocteau (right)

did not suit him. However much truth there may have been in this observation about Pasternak's egocentricity, he seems, even in those Paris days, to have had a premonition of the terror to come.

In this time of fear, when countless people were taken overnight from their homes, Pasternak met the woman who, under the name of 'Lara', was to become the chief female character in his *Dr Zhivago*. It may be that it was she who helped him to overcome the grey, intangible, nameless fear of those years. Perhaps it was this very fear which gave rise to the metamorphosis in his poetry whereby it was given a new clarity and translucence. In a passage from the continuation of *The Childhood of Luvers* which the *Literaturnaya Gazyeta* published unexpectedly in 1938, Pasternak's work shows the onset of this change, which becomes even more evident in those poems that were published during the war.

Although Pasternak was condemned by the critics, his fellow-writers obviously still believed him to be on good terms with the more important Party functionaries—or, at least, to have sufficient courage to appeal to these men. When the poet, Ossip Mandelstam was arrested, his wife turned to Boris and asked him to intervene on her husband's behalf. Pasternak did so, and the consequences were odd indeed. One day, while he was staying at a friend's country house, the telephone bell rang. It was a call from Moscow. The man who wanted to speak to Boris Pasternak was Josif Visaryonovich Stalin. He had heard that Pasternak had intervened on Mandelstam's behalf. Yes, said Boris, that was true. Did he, Pasternak, consider Mandelstam to be a great poet? Boris gave an evasive answer.

He told the man in the Kremlin that it was a good maxim never to compare one beautiful woman with another, nor one poet with another. But the caller was insistent. Pasternak thereupon confirmed that Mandelstam was a great poet deserving of protection—even though he was a poet of a different type from Pasternak himself. There the conversation ended. Some said that Pasternak blamed himself for not having put Mandelstam's case more strongly, but these were no more than rumours. What is established is that the tele-phone conversation between Stalin and Pasternak did take place.

There is another anecdote which tells how Pasternak, through an experience in the first months of the war, was able to master the fear that beset the people at that time. As an Air Raid Warden posted on the roof of the house he saw a bomb hit the next-door building. It is said that this moment, when death was so very close to him, profoundly shocked him and at the same time liberated his spirit. He saw the people streaming out of the basement of the house, grey in the fading light of day, grey from fear—whereupon those thoughts came to him to which he gave vent soon afterwards before the Writers' Associa-tion. What was there to be feared except death, and was death something so terrible? Doubtless he was himself deeply affected at that time by the thought which he put into the mouths of Dr Zhivago's two friends; namely, that the war with its deadly peril represented salvation after the agonizing and incomprehensible fears of the years that preceded it—after those fears which he described when he remembered the suicides of his friends. One of these suicides occurred in 1941 when Maria Tsvetayeva took her life. In 1935 in Paris, to which she had emigrated, she had asked Pasternak whether she should return to the Soviet Union, because she, as a poet, could not breathe in a foreign land. Boris described to her the difficulties she would have to face, but she went home nevertheless, and now he felt that he was partly to blame for her suicide.

The war interrupted every activity and everybody's thoughts were influenced by it. All the forces that could help the threatened Soviet Union had to be mobilized. Russian patriotism was given a fresh stimulus. The Russian Orthodox Church organized collections to equip a tank division. Poets who for years had been forced into silence were allowed to praise Russia's past. Even those cosmopolitans who had looked upon the intellectual life of Russia as inseparable from Europe, were at liberty to speak, whilst unpolitical lyric poetry was permitted, because it, too, could give courage and inspiration to the fighting men. The aims of the Party took second place. It even became possible to publish a small volume by Pasternak. It is called *In Early Trains* and it contains twenty-six poems, some of which touch upon subjects relating to the war. They are no flag-waving marching songs, but in their overtones one can discern his love for the suffering Russian fatherland; and

War sweeps across Russia. Villages and towns go up in flames

as the war neared its end Boris Pasternak wrote a poem, radiant with hope, called 'Spring, 1944'. The breath of spring washes away from the homeland the signs of winter, washes away the dark rings which tears had drawn around Slav eyes. Moscow was the home and the source of all that which would flower in centuries to come.

'A war is not a game of chess. It cannot simply end with the victory of white over black. Something new must come out of it. So many sacrifices cannot have been in vain.'

With thoughts such as these Pasternak welcomed the days of peace, days which for Russia were days full of victory celebrations—echoing, now in tones of thunder, now with hollow, tinny sound. The nameless fear of those grey years of the terror and the purges had given way to suffering which, though brought about by a war that was cruel and destructive, was understandable in human terms. The war years had also brought an encouraging and unexpected development, of which Dr Zhivago's friend in Pasternak's novel says, 'The tempering of the younger generation through want, their heroism, their readiness to face the great, the desperate, the fantastic, these are fabulous, astounding virtues which have now come into bloom.'

Russia, composing all internal quarrels, puts up a determined defence against the German attack

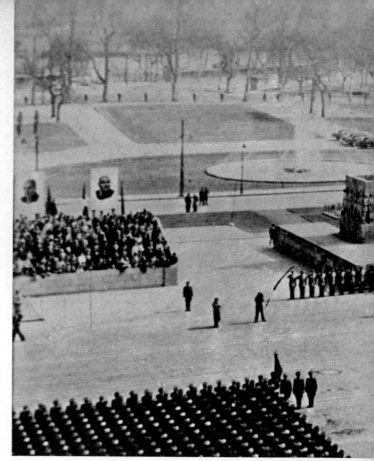

Huge monuments are a reminder of the Red Army's victory in 1945, which has been built up into a national saga. (Our photograph shows the statue of Stalin in Budapest, typical of the victory monuments in Russia and the satellite States)

No doubt the fifty-five-year-old poet was carried along on a wave of optimism in the first post-war year. The war had compelled the Communist Party to mobilize all the forces of that great country. From 1941 onwards loyalty to Stalin had no longer been the sole test of a man's convictions. He was once again allowed to give expression to a simple, patriotic love for his country, which had nothing to do with political parties. 'Cosmopolitans', 'decadents', and practising Christians had no longer to remain silent—as long as their voices helped to awaken the forces required to resist the German invasion. Many of Pasternak's friends were allowed to work and to publish, and they did so with renewed vigour. And in 1945 another small volume of Pasternak's poems was published. It comprised a few of the many poems which he had written over a period of years for himself or a few of his closest friends; yet this small volume, *The Wide Earth*, shows that not everything was composed merely for his private satisfaction. The poems, perhaps because some of them dealt with the war, were not at once attacked by the reviewers with their customary venom. The periodical *Snamya* wrote, in unusually friendly tones for a criticism of

Pasternak, 'After Pasternak had turned to the subject of war he was able to gain from this contemporary theme, overladen with the clatter of battle, a few new points of view which are wise and poetical, even if somewhat belated. Pasternak's war poems do not belong to the best of their kind, but they are motivated by love and respect for the Soviet man, the fighter, and the victor.'

These new poems were alive and direct, full of fresh insight and deep humanity. They conquered the hearts of his readers at once. They were creations of lyrical beauty, as clear as glass, as pure as crystal, and could be comprehended by those who had not been able to get much from Pasternak's previous poems, abounding as they did in symbols and newly invented words of concentrated meaning. The small volume was quickly sold out. This was confirmation to the poet that he had chosen the right way.

But the new freedom was short-lived. Critics who wrote kindly about Pasternak were reproved and put in their place. His war poems were too 'neutral and individualistic'. This was the prelude to a new gagging of Soviet literature. The Zhdanov era had begun.

Nevertheless, this firm conviction that with the war an epoch had ended and something new had begun, gave Boris Pasternak the courage to start on a new work, which he had been preparing in his mind for years. He began to write his novel *Dr Zhivago*. In the quiet of the house in Peredyelkino, amongst the encroaching fruit trees, the copse of wild firs dotted with raspberry bushes, Boris Pasternak started to work on the book that was to put on record, for himself and for his people, the great and terrible years through which he lived.

It was like an act of self-deliverance, a coming to terms with those years of unresolved history which are officially taboo for Soviet literature to this day. For terror, suffering and human want must remain hidden in the shadow of that imposing memorial which, in gleaming white marble, symbolizes the Revolution. But nobody who had lived through these times could really forget that which officialdom decreed should remain in the shadow. Pasternak, for his part, could not keep silent. He had to find an outlet for such feelings lest he be suffocated by them—this man who among all his literary friends and foes was practically the only one to survive the years of purges. This work, he confessed some years later, helped him to overcome a mental crisis. Perhaps it was the crisis of the esoteric lyrical writer, who in his 'spiritual emigration' wrote poems that were not meant to be published. Perhaps it was the nagging conscience of one who had translated great European classics, and had survived the era of terror in relatively comfortable circumstances; a conscience which forced him to work on his *Dr Zhivago*.

'After the war I learned that I have a reputation with some people—that there are people even abroad, who know the name of Boris Pasternak, and so I said to myself, "You must stand to attention before your own name." I said to myself that I must first deserve this name—not by poems, but by prose, by something which would cost me more work, effort, time and perhaps even something else.' That is what Pasternak told me when describing his emotions as he started to write *Dr Zhivago*. And as he spoke, the tall elderly man with his narrow angular face, his almost white hair that was always a little untidy, his shining grey eyes, jumped up and stood to attention, his hands at the seams of his trouser-legs. Ten years later he still seemed to be experiencing the feeling of relief which the beginning of his first, and perhaps only, long novel had brought him.

No sooner did he begin to write than the sky darkened once more. There was little chance of seeing the growing book ever published. Yet, shortly before the hand of the Party ideologist, Andrei Zhdanov, again descended heavily on the spiritual life of the Soviet Union, Pasternak had an experience which must have given him courage and strength for the difficult years ahead. In a public gathering of the Writers' Association he was allowed to step once more on to the platform at the side of the other writers. His colleagues had earned moderate applause. When Pasternak appeared he was given an enthusiastic ovation.

Boris Pasternak in the early post-war years

They asked him to read his poems. When he had finished, his listeners asked for more. Pasternak was not prepared for this. He tried to recite some of them from memory, but even while doing so his voice failed, so moved and touched was he. Whenever the poet on the platform came to a halt all the people in the hall continued the thread of words, reciting in chorus the works of the speechless poet. With tears in his eyes Pasternak called out to the crowd, 'Spassibo, dorogyie'—'Thank you, dear ones!'

This happened at a time when Pasternak's poems were nowhere to be bought. Friends passed on handwritten copies. Furthermore, the poems endured in the memories of men whose hunger for the human word could not be assuaged by the literature then being printed. Ilya Ehrenburg may have had this in mind when he discussed poetry in the Soviet Union with some of his foreign friends. When he was asked about Pasternak he answered, 'Pasternak's poems are not for sale here at the moment. It appears that there is no interest in them—but if Pasternak would announce one day that he is giving a public reading of his poems, I believe that twenty thousand people would come from all corners of Russia, on foot if necessary, just to be present at that gathering.'

Since that appearance ten years ago Boris Pasternak has not stepped on to a public platform. What is more, his work on *Dr Zhivago* had to be postponed. A new wave of persecu

Andrei Zhdanov, a member of the Central Committee of the Soviet Communist Party, and the leading ideologist of the Party in matters pertaining to art

tions began. Some of the writers who were arrested had pages of the manuscript of *Dr Zhivago* in their possession—but, again, nothing happened to its author. He lived in that calm which is to be found at the centre of every whirlwind.

Nevertheless the Soviet Writers' Association was reprimanded by the Central Committee of the Party for the publication of Pasternak's poems. The *Literaturnaya Gazyeta*, the organ of the Association, put the blame on to the Management Committee, and said that they were responsible for the publication of Pasternak's poetry, which was 'unpolitical, devoid of ideas, alien to the people'. The First Secretary of the Association, Aleksei Fadeyev, ~Alexander~ Boris's neighbour in the writer's colony of Peredjelkino, went over to the attack: he maintained that although his colleague had grown up under the Soviet regime he had remained an individualist, whose work was utterly alien to the spirit of Soviet society. Ten years later, when Fadeyev—who was both Stalin's tool and his victim—committed suicide, that same neighbour whom he had once admonished wrote with understanding, even pity, of this man who had concealed his insidious political machinations behind a somewhat self-conscious smirk.

The critics and the writers who had taken Pasternak's side during the war and in the first post-war years, had had to indulge in some self-criticism since 1946. Soviet literature

Ilya Ehrenburg—a striking personality in the fluctuations of Soviet policy with regard to literature

had been subjected once more to an intensified censorship by Zhdanov. Whereupon Paster-nak resumed his translations. He undertook a task which demanded all his strength: the translation of both parts of Goethe's *Faust*.

Numerous Russian translations of *Faust* already existed. The new attempt was a gigantic enterprise which could only be undertaken successfully by one who, over and above a gift for poetic transliteration, possessed a deep understanding of Goethe. The manner in which Pasternak solved this problem would alone be a yardstick of his status as a poet. So free and at the same time so faithful a rendering of *Faust* could only be achieved by a man who has found his spiritual home beyond the confines of national literatures (which, seen in this perspective, seem to be almost provincial), where the current of world literature flows most strongly.

Without clinging to individual words, yet keeping to the essence of what Goethe says in every line, he was sometimes amazingly faithful in form and word sequence, and at other times he created something new out of the Goethean spirit. So it was that a work of art was born, which belongs to the sublimest in the annals of translations of great litera-ture. Precise but not pedantic, Pasternak's version of *Faust* is (particularly for the German reader who remembers the original from his school days only too well) a fascinating new encounter with Goethe's work. The vast pile of commentaries, interpretations and analyses to the second part of the tragedy, produced by German literary research scholars alone,

Aleksei Fadeyev, for many years First Secretary of the Soviet Writers' Association, was one of Pasternak's neighbours in Peredjelkino. He took his own life in May, 1956

The board of directors of the Moscow Arts Theatre (from left to right: olodovnikov, Stanitsin, Raevsky), where Pasternak's translations of plays by Shakespeare, Goethe and Schiller (most recently, *Mary Stuart*) have been frequently presented

shows very clearly with what problems the translator has to cope. He had to convey in another language passages which remain a puzzle even for specialists in German philology. Pasternak left out some of these passages—realizing that he must not try to translate what he did not understand. Other verses he sagaciously and carefully clarified, but never at the expense of their poetry or their content, and always without weakening the power of the poetic word by intellectual explanations and elucidations. In the words of Pasternak himself, who sometimes seems to speak of Shakespeare and Goethe as if they were much loved and admired contemporaries, 'There are passages in the first and second

Historical personalities of the Moscow Arts Theatre: Stanislavsky (left) and Nemirovich-Danchenko

parts of *Faust* which conquer us by the poetry. For minutes it is as if we were unconscious; yet, however often and carefully we read them over, we are unable to say what it is about them that conquers and delights us.' Here we can recognize the root of the strength that has enabled Boris Pasternak to survive even the most heartbreaking years of his life without hatred, bitterness and prejudice . . . yet at the same time the future did hold a promise— 'To have before us so much difficult and happy work. The aim is so simple—to bring back the living spirit of highminded nobility to the realm of human relations, and to carry it on into the future.'

In the difficult years during and just after the war Zinaida Pasternak tried to protect her husband as well as she could from the material difficulties of life. Now that their circle of guests had grown and the shops and market stalls were slowly filling again, she could lay the large dining-table once more. Her husband made fun of her: 'It is in the nature of

A scene from Schiller's *Maria Stuart* at the Moscow Drama Theatre, in Pasternak's Russian rendering

beavers to build dams wherever they may be. You could shut a beaver up in a bedroom, and he would immediately start building a dam. It is very similar in the case of my wife: whether we expect guests or not, every Sunday she prepares a huge midday meal, and I have to sit glued to the phone, inviting people to help us eat all that food.'

Boris Pasternak loved to invite people, he loved to play the host, and to talk with his guests. On such occasions he would get up again and again, sparkling with vivacity and enthusiasm, to raise his glass of Armenian brandy in a toast. He would laugh, gesticulate, and throw new thoughts and remarks that were jocular yet serious into the conversation. His hair was nearly white, but this slim, volatile man did not give the impression of someone who was approaching seventy. Sometimes there was a shadow of melancholy over his shining eyes, a soft, sad expression on his full lips, but his angular face radiated creative strength, vitality and passion, and there was hardly anyone who could escape its magic. In

Stalin, whose name is associated with the terrible purges, died on March 5, 1953. He lies in state, next to Lenin, in the Mausoleum outside the walls of the Kremlin. The triumvirate, Malenkov, Bulganin and Khrushchev (below, from right to left) take over the government

the seventh decade of his life Boris Pasternak appeared to be almost younger than his son, Leonid, and his son's contemporaries who were still going to school. Something of the grand, gay, adventurous craziness of the early years of the world of modern art, the memory of which still clung to Pasternak, seemed to return.

Yet he had no real reason for such carefree lightheartedness. The thaw had started, but the new Spring of Russian literature had not yet arrived. In 1954, before Ehrenburg's novel had caused the more liberal-minded phase to be labelled 'the thaw', the literary paper *Znamya* printed ten poems by Pasternak, under the title 'Verses from the Novel in Prose, Dr Zhivago'. The poems were prefaced by a short note by the poet: 'The novel will probably be finished in the summer. It deals with the period from 1906 to 1929, and contains an epilogue which refers to the great war fought for our fatherland. Its hero, Yury Andreyevitch Zhivago, a meditative and ever-searching doctor, with creative and artistic interests, dies in 1929. He leaves notes and papers, among them verses which he wrote in his youth. These verses of which some are printed here constitute the final chapter of the novel.'

Pasternak thought that, at last, the time was ripe to present the public with *Dr Zhivago*. The optimism with which he had started years ago to write a long novel, apparently only to have to put it aside, seemed justified. Actually it was too early even for the poems. In the summer of 1954 their author was again attacked in *Pravda*. The poems from his novel caused him to be called, once again, a decadent, a symbolist and a subjectivist individualist. Two years went by without a single line of his being printed in the Soviet Union.

The seclusion of his study, into which only very rarely a newspaper brought the echo of bustling officialdom, was invaded occasionally by the arrival of semi-official commissions, which Pasternak did not refuse to see. There was indeed no need for him to do so, because they did not demand from him anything that he found unbearable. In 1955 the German writer, Bertolt Brecht, requested that no one but Pasternak should translate the speech in which he, in May, was to give thanks in Moscow for the award of the Stalin Prize. Pasternak translated the speech without real enjoyment; similarly, he found little pleasure in the volume of poems by the same author, which had been published in Eastern Germany, and which Brecht had presented to him. He commented that he had no affinity with poets who were

Pasternak and his wife Zinaida were generous hosts. As the paralysing effect of the Stalin era wore off the poet's house in Peredjelkino began again to fill with cheerful guests

Beneath a portrait of Picasso: Ilya Ehrenburg (third from left, between the Armenian painter, Saruyan, and the bearded sculptor, Konenko), the title of whose novel *The Thaw* was used to describe the long-awaited liberalization of living conditions in the Soviet Union

primarily political. It was only some years later, when Helene Weigel came to Moscow with the 'Berlin Ensemble', that he discovered that the selection of purely political poems had made it difficult for him to see what a great poet Brecht was. The splendour of the reception in honour of the Stalin Prize winner, Brecht, failed to lure Pasternak to Moscow.

Quietly he went on working. From the window of his study on the first floor one can see across wide open fields to a distant wood. The shadows of its trees fall along the crosses of the Peredjelkino cemetery. The onion-shaped spires of the Orthodox Church glitter light blue, and the air is often filled with the sound of the plaintive singing of Christian mourners on their way to the little cemetery. Later, perhaps, there will be accordion-playing as the mourners find their way back to the land of the living. Sometimes the peace is broken by the muted brass of funerals where an atheist is buried according to the rites of the new society. The funeral marches are monotonously disconsolate on the way to the cemetery, but on the way back the brass bands sound relieved, and sometimes slightly uncertain because of the funeral libations. Hymns, brass bands, or accordion, their sound alters the mystery of death as little as resolutions can explain the mystery of life or directives change the substance of it.

The poet in his seventh decade knew this, and he knew also that he himself had to speak his mind.

Meanwhile the thaw continued. The Soviet writers came to grips with the reality of their existence in poems, short stories, novels and essays. They did not wish to attack the foundation of the Soviet system. All they wanted was to improve it by remedying faults, hardships, and abuses. They wished to help the Party to remit the mortgage of fear and injustice which Stalin had left behind, and of which it was now possible to speak with ever-increasing frankness. Young Soviet readers were fascinated and inspirited by this new freedom of speech, in which writers and critics came perilously, though unintentionally, close to transgressing the limits laid down for them by the Party.

Boris Pasternak did not participate in the ups and downs of the quarrel between the reformists and the orthodox. He was left alone. The Party functionaries who concerned themselves with literature had perhaps by now forgotten the Zhivago poems. In New York the head of the Foreign Branch of the Writers' Association, Boris Polevoy, maintained that he had never heard of a novel by Pasternak. A Soviet journalist remarked that Boris Pasternak

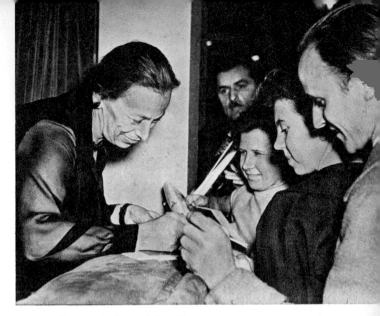

1957: Helene Weigel, Brecht's wife, on tour in Moscow, signing autographs

had not finished his novel because his translation work made him 'rich and indolent'.

The year 1955 came to an end. *Dr Zhivago* was completed.

In the Spring and Summer of 1956, when the Hungarian revolution brought about the great change of climate, many works, which were criticized and condemned by the Party, were published. But *Dr Zhivago* was not among them. The editorial board of the periodical *Novy Mir* (who later called down upon themselves Khrushchev's disfavour by publishing the novel *Not By Bread Alone* by Dudintsev) rejected Pasternak's work. In a long letter, which was obviously the result of serious thought and discussion, the editorial board explained why Pasternak's new novel should not be published in the Soviet Union. The letter was written without animosity. Rather, it had an element of regret and anxiety, even though it did also contain a few satirical sentences which were full of petty viciousness. But this letter, which bore the signature of Pasternak's friend and neighbour, the famous epic poet, Constantin Fedin, shows clearly how much the discussion among Soviet writers even then differed from the narrow-minded uproar at the literary show-trials—although even at this stage, even in this, the only serious criticism of *Dr Zhivago* in the Soviet Union, differences of opinion were already tending towards bitterness. The opposing points of view are obvious: on the one side are men who do not want to give up the hope that planned and guided efforts can bring about a change in the material living conditions of a new and better man, in a new and better community. On the other side stands a man who firmly believes that the value of human life cannot be measured with theories, dogmas and ideologies; a man who dares to believe that real innovation must come slowly. He is not scornful of the successes

When Bertolt Brecht received the Stalin Peace Prize in 1955 (he is seen here with N. S. Tikhinov) he asked Pasternak to translate his speech of thanks into Russian

In 1956 Vladimir Dudintsev was reprimanded by the Party for his novel *Not by Bread Alone*

In 1956 the 'thaw' ended. The Moscow magazine *Krokodil* ridiculed the 'Individualist writers': 'What are you writing there? Your thesis?' —'Ssh! A novel!'

and accomplishments reflected in the statistics of the State plans, but his scale of values is different. Time and time again Boris Pasternak told friends and acquaintances, who complained and criticized this or that decision of the Soviet government: 'The time for proclamations, outcries, and excitement is in reality over. Now something else is growing. It is growing inconspicuously and silently like grass. It is growing like a fruit; it is growing imperceptibly in the children. The real significance of this epoch is that in it a new freedom is beginning.'

This is not the creed of a literary insurgent. These are not the words of a partisan in the struggle for or against Capitalism, Socialism or Communism. From the place which Pasternak has won for himself, half a century seems a very small fragment of the eternal flow of life. He is no Marxist, no Communist; but, then, which party could claim as a member a man who looks upon the passing centuries as the footsteps of God, and who regards the Russian Revolution and the developments which grew out of it, as but an intermediary phase of world history, leading to something new? What he says of his novel is true: 'I have borne witness as an artist. I have described how the ages have affected me, but this is no accusation against Soviet society. I am telling you this in all frankness.'

When, in spite of everything, the book became a political sensation, when it even caused an international political scandal, it was not its author's fault. Those who were guilty were the narrow-minded literary bureaucrats, who, using their usual sledgehammer-methods, went to other countries to prevent the publication of the novel. At the time when the manuscript was being read and examined in various editorial offices of magazines and book publishers in Moscow, the Communist publisher Feltrinelli, in Italy, received a copy of it. He had also got a contract with a six months' embargo on publication. During that time a young Communist editor in Moscow was to make the cuts in the novel which were necessary for a Soviet edition. Pasternak had agreed to such cuts. On the wall of his study above the high desk at which he works, hang the originals of the illustrations which his father, Leonid Pasternak, did for Leo Tolstoy's *Resurrection*. When Tolstoy's book was published, the first edition of the work was only allowed to be printed in a censored and shortened form, but, regardless of all cuts, Tolstoy's *Resurrection* was still a great work. Boris Pasternak knew this. He knew in what kind of a State he lived, and he would have had no objection to his

Konstantin Fedin, one of Pasternak's neighbours in Peredjelkino, was in 1956 opposed to the publication of the novel *Dr Zhivago*

own book being shortened. He did say, however, that he was not one of those authors who were engaged day and night in rewriting their own books according to Party specifications. He was firmly convinced that a shortened edition of *Dr Zhivago* would be published in the Soviet Union.

But his manuscript remained unprinted, in the hands of the publishers. Each department passed on the responsibility to the one above it, and, in the end, nobody could be found who felt himself to be in a strong enough position to authorize publication. The publisher in Milan was again asked to postpone the publication of the novel in Italy. During this time Pasternak himself was ill in the so-called Kremlin-clinic, a hospital for particularly prominent citizens of the Soviet Union, because of his old knee injury, which began to worry him again in his old age. Even if his own creative work was dismissed as valueless, the health of Pasternak the translator was taken good care of.

In his bed in the Kremlin-clinic Pasternak saw time drifting away without a decision about the novel being taken, and Feltrinelli was not willing to wait any longer. He knew nothing of a shortened Soviet edition. He was resolved to publish *Dr Zhivago*. In Moscow the members of the executive of the Writers' Association approached Pasternak, and suggested to him, amiably but urgently, that he should send a cable to Feltrinelli, and ask the Italian publisher to return the manuscript. As a reason for this request, he should say that he wanted to make a few improvements in it. Pasternak did not have much faith in the effect of such a cable, but he sent it off.

As could have been foreseen, Feltrinelli insisted on his contractual rights. He was not prepared to postpone once again the publication of the book. It was at this juncture that the Soviet Embassy in Rome, and the First Secretary of the Soviet Writers' Association began that course of action which was to turn the publication of a great poetic novel into a political sensation. In Milan, Aleksei Surkov tried to put pressure on Feltrinelli who, after all, as a member of the Communist Party, owed a certain obedience to the Party, but Surkov, Member of the Central Committee of the Soviet Communist Party, and pivot of the literary life of the Party, was not properly prepared for negotiations with Italian Communists. The efforts of this sturdy man, with his loud orator's voice, had a most unexpected result: the Italian Communist Party lost the extremely wealthy Milan publisher, who had been one of their most profitable members—and the novel *Dr Zhivago*, of which until then hardly anything was known in the West, began to attract attention even before publication.

In the preceding years one could often have found people from other countries among the guests in Pasternak's country house: young people who studied in Moscow, or left-wing

With the suppression of the Hungarian uprising in November 1956 the time of alleviation came to an end

writers who were visiting the Soviet Union, and who saw in Pasternak's existence a means of alleviating their doubts concerning the position of intellectuals in the Soviet Union. However, the official Soviet intervention in Milan placed Pasternak's name on the front pages of newspapers in the West, and now journalists from many countries requested to be allowed to interview Boris Pasternak. The 'State Committee for Cultural Relations with Foreign

Aleksei Surkov, First Secretary of the Soviet Writers' Association, tried in vain to prevent the publication of the novel *Dr Zhivago* in Italy

Countries' arranged that two groups of foreign correspondents should see for themselves how unmolested Pasternak's life was.

I no longer remember what sort of a reception I expected in 1957 when I visited Boris Pasternak for the first time. But I certainly did not expect to find him laughing and waving from the steps of his house. I had thought that I would find that atmosphere of caution and distrust which the foreigner encounters everywhere in the Soviet Union.

I stepped through a narrow door out of the sharp winter's cold into the warm kitchen. Pasternak took both my hands in his while I introduced myself in Russian, and then he laughed. 'So you are the correspondent from Western Germany I was expecting', he said. And then he added in German: 'So jung und schon so verdorben' (So young and already so spoiled). This is a German saying which he remembered from his youth, and which appealed to him. He repeated it when later, glass in hand, he proposed a toast.

After a welcome which lasted some minutes, and which was as chaotic as it was jovial, I found myself in the poet's study on the first floor. His wife led us into the light, almost

The Milan publisher, Feltrinelli
was not to be deterred by
appeals and threats
from Moscow from pub-
lishing the novel *Dr Zhivago*
in Italy

empty room with its large windows. There was a desk, a light wardrobe, next to which were
a few cases, a couple of wooden chairs and a narrow dark-stained bookshelf containing a
small reference library. In this a large English-Russian dictionary stood next to a thick
Russian Bible. There was almost the entire German edition of Kafka's works, and, in
French, Marcel Proust's *À la Recherche du Temps Perdu*. Pasternak then said, 'I have never
read Kafka; I have only recently got his books. I am reading Proust at the moment. Very
good. Sometimes very, very good. But something is missing. Well, we will talk about it
later.' Now began, almost without any transition, a stormy soliloquy. It was an attempt by
the poet to give an account of himself, to define his work and its boundaries. Names came
and went in a whirl of comparisons—Rilke, Thomas Mann, T. S. Eliot, James Joyce. 'To
combine the power of Thomas Mann with that of Rilke—what a work of art that would
produce.' Thomas Mann was too much of the experimental psychologist and the literary
review essayist. But his art combined with the sensitivity and depth, with that feeling for
the transcendental of the Rilke who wrote *Malte Laurids Brigge*—that would be something!

Pasternak's 'dacha' (country house) in Peredjelkino

And what a novel James Joyce's *Ulysses* would be if it also had the clarity of the stories in the *Dubliners*! Pasternak said that he was a modern man, and almost apologized for his high desk, which, although it did remind him of Goethe, he used because of his ailing leg. He explained that he had to work in the world of contemporary forms. It differed from the art world of earlier times. In the same way, in Goethe's work one could find reflections of all the currents of his time, sometimes over-individualistic and over-topical, but never a mere personal avowal, or impressionist sketch. Then, all of a sudden, out of the whirl of comment on world literature, we began to speak about *Dr Zhivago*. This was just the time when the book was being published in Italy, and when the first sensational reports and the first attacks were being made in the papers of foreign Communist parties.

'I am not sorry that my novel has been published in the West,' Pasternak told me, 'but I regret all the fuss that has been made over it. Everybody is writing about it. But who has actually read the book? What do they quote from it? Always the same three pages from a book of seven hundred pages.' He looked at me questioningly. Had I, by any chance, read his book? I had not read it. I do not know any Italian, and, in any case, there was no Italian edition of the book to be had in the whole of Moscow at that time. Not even Pasternak himself had yet seen his book in print. The fuss about it was all that had reached him. He repudiated nothing. There was not a sentence in his novel that he would strike out, not a word. But then, and later too, he protested against his book being regarded as a political

Pasternak in
front of
his 'dacha'

pamphlet, a document of accusation against the society in which he lived. Soon the propagandists would be describing Pasternak's novel as the product of a damned counter-revolutionary, or that of a saintly anti-communist. But when Boris Pasternak says that his book is not the work of a politician he speaks with conviction. He takes little interest in ideological controversies. On the other hand, he certainly is no Communist. He makes no secret of the fact that he does not believe in dialectical materialism. In casual conversation he described himself as 'almost an atheist'. After which he unfolded his concept of God with deep emotion. He said that man can feel the presence of the Divine, deeply and clearly, perhaps three, and certainly not more than ten, times in his whole life—in his love of a work of art, in his love of a woman, in his love of his country . . . and downstairs in the dining-room at the long table covered with a white table-cloth, he spoke again of this love for his country. He called for a patriotic toast, and, while his friends waited for him to speak, he raised his glass of vodka: he said that he must be grateful to his epoch and his country, for it was by this epoch and this country that his life and work had been shaped. In another toast he drank to the literary guidance given by the Soviet State. He had been an esoteric poet, lost in phantasies and sensations, and he was grateful for this education: 'I have not become a socialist realist,' he said, 'no, certainly not a socialist realist. But I have become a realist, and for that I am grateful.'

His listeners may well have asked themselves whether this transformation from a writer of lyrical and abstruse verses to a realistic prose writer had in fact been the result of the Writers' Association's educational activities; or whether it had not rather been the result of great emotional upheavals which had found no room for expression in the artistic, individual, and occasionally precious lyrics of earlier years. Soviet critics said of him that he lived in an ivory tower, that he was afraid of reality, but the novel *Dr Zhivago* was to burst the walls of the ivory tower. It was to be a simple document, understandable to all. Pasternak compared it to Grimmelshausen's *Simplizissimus*, even to *Uncle Tom's Cabin*.

It was precisely this change to simplicity and universal intelligibility that infuriated officials in the literary department of the Party, and that made them declare that the new novel might damage Pasternak's reputation as a poet. It was easier for them to endure a man whom they could reproach for living in an ivory tower, than to tolerate a great poet who was facing his own era in a realistic novel. This coming to grips with the situation, which so terrified them, was for Pasternak an act of self-liberation, of deliverance from the shadows of the past, which it was absolutely necessary for him to undertake. But the reproach that he is a propagandist of the reactionary past, or of the capitalist enemies of his country, can touch Pasternak as little as the false praise of those who see in him an ally of capitalism. His

The poet at his writing desk

Pasternak's guests mu[st]
have strong heads. Over and ov[er]
again the poet proposes new toas[ts]

philosophy of life is very far removed from this kind of controversy. He once told a Swedish literary scholar: 'In the nineteenth century power was held by the middle classes. You have read about it in books and perceived it even better, perhaps, in Ibsen's plays. People looked for security in money or possessions. Man's dream of security was strong and unshakable, but now he has realized that there is no security for him. This is not only a Russian experience. In an era of world wars, in an atomic age, these things have lost their meaning for him. We have learned: we are life's guests, travellers between two stations. We must seek our security within ourselves. In our short lives, we must make up our minds about our relationship to the world in which we live, about our place in the universe. This means, as I see it, to turn away from the materialist philosophy of the nineteenth century. It means a renaissance of spiritual values, of religion. By this I do not mean religion as a dogma, nor as a Church that has no vitality. Do you see what I mean?'

No, the man who speaks like this does not live in a world of ideological controversies. His point of view towards his environment and the society in which he lives may appear strange and ambiguous, but this is not merely a result of the difficult position in which an exceptional poet finds himself in the Soviet Union. This poet, with his extreme vitality and optimism, and his profound belief in the forces of life, refuses either to take up arms against the world around him, or to retire in bitterness from that world. His is the voice of the Russia which is still faithful to the world of Russian Classical literature— of a Russia which is today hidden from us by the gigantic façade of technical development and the grey backdrop of

ideological newspaper articles. Perhaps he may be the voice of the 'other' Russia, but he certainly does not speak for the world which crumbled to pieces in the great Revolution. The Russia for which Pasternak speaks has been shaped just as much by the four decades after the Revolution as by the centuries of Tsarist and Church rule before it. But he feels that in the society and the State in which his work is being considered merely as an annoyance a new epoch is growing—'inconspicuously and silently like grass'.

The panorama of Moscow: the Soviet Union's

This hope is not based on the liberalization of Soviet domestic policy. It is true that life has become easier and more pleasant, for Pasternak too, since the terror of the Stalin era faded away, but so far as his work is concerned, nothing much has changed. Some of his poems were allowed to appear in the periodicals *Znamya* and *Novy Mir*, and a few were published in the verse anthology, *Day of Poetry*, but that was all that was allowed to appear, even in 1956, during the first six months of which writers were able to speak with greater freedom than in the twenty previous years.

The publication of a collection of Pasternak's lyrical poems was in preparation, and the poet wrote a long and detailed preface—his second autobiographical study. But the book did not appear. The thaw had passed its peak before the preparations were completed, and on May 14, 1957 the executive of the Writers' Association met in its third plenary session, to define anew the limits within which poets and writers, after years of ideological uncertainty, were to remain. There was no return to the hard, narrow-minded precepts which Andrei Zhdanov had laid down ten years ago, but literature was again given instructions for its mission—to assist the Party. The main targets of this attack were the younger critics of the system. But Pasternak's work was not spared either. Lyrical poets are also dangerous,

splendid façade of bold town planning

stated the critic Alexander Dymshitz. And he gave a warning against reprinting the works of Maria Tsvetayeva or Osip Mandelstam. He even admitted, with a certain amount of circumlocution, that the poems of the futurist, Velemir Khlebnikov, who had died thirty-five years previously from want and starvation, were still being read by young people—and declared that this was bad for them! As was to be expected, the name of the living poet followed after the names of his dead friends. Dymshitz said, 'I remember how much the poems in *The Year 1905* and *Lieutenant Schmidt* used to mean to all of us. But the path which Pasternak has taken since then has grieved us—and still does so.'

The man from whom the younger generation had to be protected lived quietly and in seclusion in his house at Peredjelkino. He took no part in literary-political discussions. He seldom visited his flat in Moscow. Boris Pasternak's health was not very good, but the year 1957 would, in any case, not have been a year of important work for him. He, and more especially his wife, felt the strained atmosphere while his novel *Dr Zhivago* was being scrutinized by Soviet officials, and even more so while it was being printed in Italy. And yet nothing happened. The poet's house was surrounded by a silence, seemingly peaceful and yet, at the same time, ominous.

The fluctuations of the Party line gave the Soviet writers an ever-increasing sense of insecurity. *Krokodil* mockingly comments, 'The dramatist is not in his study. In calm weather he doesn't work at all'

Neither the Press nor the literary magazines of the Soviet Union mentioned the existence of the novel *Dr Zhivago*. It seemed that nobody wanted to bring it up for discussion. There was no decision as to what conclusions were to be drawn from the publication of the novel abroad. Perhaps it was the memory of the literary and political purges of the Stalin era, when the witch-hunt had not spared the hunters themselves, that restrained even the most ardent Communists. The miseries of those years were not forgotten even by those who had implicit faith in the Party. Among them were people who tried to help Pasternak, and again it became clear that this man, much too frank and much too honest though he was, had almost no enemies. He was spared being dragged into the political arguments of the Press and Party, but it was impossible to prevent the highest authorities of the Party from occupying themselves with him.

A satirical cartoon in *Krokodil* on
the publication of *Dr Zhivago* in the West.
The editor of a scandal
sheet says about the novel,
'This is a clean job!'

According to an anecdote which made the rounds in Moscow, Nikita Khrushchev himself had been given a report on Boris Pasternak in the early summer of 1958 by one of the
two writers who were members of the Party's Central Committee. The various versions of
the story differ as to whether it was the First Secretary of the Writers' Association, Aleksei
Surkov, or the old peasant-poet, Feodor Panferov—but they all agree on what was said on
that occasion.

After Khrushchev had heard of the Italian edition, his first question was whether the book
had been a success. He was told that it was a success, and further translations into other
languages were to be expected. Khrushchev listened with great interest. Then he said—and
anyone who knows him can well believe the story—'But this is very interesting. Why don't
we send Pasternak to Baku for a time? He's been in the Caucasus before. Fine! Let him

tell us how the life of the workers in the oil-fields has changed since the Revolution. Such a novel would surely be of great interest to foreigners.'

To a foreign observer this may seem absurd. It is like sending T. S. Eliot into a Scottish mine, or Herman Hesse into a German steel mill, and making them write socio-political propaganda novels. It is true, however, that Boris Pasternak was urged to go to Baku. The fact that he did not have to do so, was probably due to his ill-health. His fellow-writers not only understood full well when Pasternak showed no enthusiasm for this task, but they also felt that it would be better if writers were not sent to isolated places against their wills. There were many forces working together to save Pasternak from the worst fate.

In the Spring of 1958 came the first signs that the world's highest literary honour was to come to Boris Pasternak. Albert Camus, the last holder of the Nobel Prize for Literature, was one of the first to send Boris Pasternak encouraging and sympathetic letters. The number of letters grew. More and more sentences such as, 'See you perhaps in Stockholm in the autumn,' appeared in these letters. Nor was it a secret to the Soviet Writers' Association that Boris Pasternak was on the list of candidates for the Nobel Prize. As early as January the

Association's Secretary, Surkov, had expressed annoyance at the possibility that Pasternak might receive the Nobel Prize. Pasternak, he said, was a talented poet, but the quality of his novel could not be compared with that of his earlier work. He gave no indication, however, that the official reaction to the novel would be so sharply antagonistic.

In the late Summer of 1958 the Swedish Academy put out feelers to test the mood of the Soviets, but it learned very little. There was still no official line, and the man to whom the Swedish delegates had turned for information may himself have been waiting for official guidance. The head of the Foreign Department of the Writers' Association, Boris Polevoy, had not been instructed in how to answer questions. He spoke in general terms; the novel *Dr Zhivago* was considered in the Soviet Union as insincere and without value, but there was nothing to be said against Pasternak himself. Polevoy uttered no word of warning, and gave no indication that the award of the Nobel Prize to Pasternak could possibly be regarded as an insult to the Soviet Union. But, then, what could Polevoy say? He probably knew just as little of all that was to come later, as the man for whom the great honour was to become almost a tragedy.

The publication of the Italian
edition of *Dr Zhivago*
by Feltrinelli (left)
caused a world sensation. The
West became aware of Boris Pasternak.
When Khrushchev was
told of Pasternak's success,
he wanted to send the poet
to Baku so that he could
write a novel about the
workers in the oilfields

The winner of the 1957 Nobel Prize for Literature, Albert Camus, thought, early in 1958, that Pasternak was the most promising candidate for the next Nobel Prize award

During those uneasy days Pasternak was surrounded by cheerful and sympathetic friends. As things were he could do nothing but wait. On the morning of October 23 neighbours came to report that they had heard a foreign radio station announce that Boris Pasternak was the most likely person to receive the Nobel Prize for Literature. It was practically certain that it would be awarded to him that afternoon. Dark clouds hung over the autumnal landscape at Peredjelkino. When at last the Secretary of the Swedish Academy in Stockholm announced its decision, Boris Pasternak in Peredjelkino put on his overcoat and his old cap and went out into the pouring rain. This is how he was found, walking along a narrow path through the woods, when the correspondents came from Moscow to congratulate and interview him. But he had nothing much to tell them. He thanked them for their congratulations; he did not hide his joy, but he apologized for not being able to talk with them for longer. He explained that he could think best while walking, and he must walk some more and think some more.

Pasternak in the spring of 1958 after a grave illness

The Nobel Prize Committee of the Swedish Royal Academy in Stockholm

The news that Pasternak had been awarded the Nobel Prize spread like wildfire. Neighbours and colleagues came to congratulate him. The white-haired poet Nikolai Chukovsky *Korne*
gallantly kissed Zinaida Pasternak's hand before he sat down to take a drink in celebration of the occasion. 'Infinitely grateful, moved, proud, astonished, unworthy,' these
were the words of gratitude in the cable with which Boris Pasternak expressed his feelings
on the first day. On that first day after the award no shadow clouded the joy of his friends.
But nobody who knew conditions in the Soviet Union could have felt such unrestrained
optimism as did the many foreign admirers, whose congratulatory telegrams arrived in
Peredjelkino. Yet the words uttered by the Soviet Minister of Culture on that same first
day made the earlier fears appear somewhat exaggerated. He repeated more or less what
Polevoy had already said, namely that the novel was weak but Pasternak was a good poet
and a great translator. It would, perhaps, have been more understandable if he had received
the prize ten years previously for his earlier work.

After these words there seemed to be no further occasion for anxiety and doubt. But already the first move to launch the Press campaign against Pasternak was in preparation.

Ivan Bunin, prior to Pasternak the only Russian to win the Nobel Prize for Literature (1933)

Already before the award of the Nobel Prize Pasternak received hundreds of congratulatory telegrams

The *Literaturnaya Gazyeta*, the official organ of the Writers' Association, printed a leading article, loaded with abuse, against that member of the Association who had been honoured by the Nobel Prize, and whose name had until that time often been cited in conversation with foreigners as an example of the tolerance and generosity of Soviet literary policy. The novel *Dr Zhivago*, which had been rejected by the editorial board of the periodical *Novy Mir* in a reasonable and decent manner, was now pronounced to be an 'evil-smelling libel'. The award of the Nobel Prize to Pasternak was called an act of 'carefully planned ideological agitation' against the Soviet Union. The article went on menacingly: 'The dreamer Zhivago, a narrow-minded and evil petty-bourgeois, is just as alien to the Soviet people as is that spiteful literary snob, Pasternak himself. He is their enemy, and the ally of those who hate our country and our way of life. The "ovation" which the West have given him confirms this clearly. . . . He has put a weapon into the hands of the enemy, and he has given

After the award: enthusiastic friends come to congratulate the poet

to bourgeois publishers this book of his which is permeated through and through with an anti-Soviet spirit. Pasternak's "world-wide" fame is confined to those who never miss a chance to slander the Soviet Union and her social and political development. But one must march either with those who seek to further Communism or with those who want to stop its progress. Pasternak has made his choice. He has chosen the path of shame and dishonour.'

This was the first reaction to the award of the Nobel Prize to a Soviet poet.

What came later no one in the West thought possible, and only a few in the Soviet Union thought probable. The campaign against the poet grew from day to day. The *Literaturnaya Gazyeta* printed, under the heading 'Anger and Disgust' a special column of readers' letters reeking of hatred—letters by people who frankly admitted that they had never read *Dr Zhivago*, but who condemned its author all the more vigorously. The climax was yet to come. In a mass meeting in the presence of Nikita Khrushchev, the leader of the

While the poet walked in his garden and thought things over, the Press was embarking on a campaign against Pasternak. The West was almost unanimously on his side, ignorant of the consequences this would have

пролетарии всех стран, соединяйтесь!

Коммунистическая партия Советского Союза

ПРАВДА

Орган Центрального Комитета
Коммунистической партии Советского Союза

Год издания 47-й № 302 (14696) Среда, 29 октября 1958 года ЦЕНА 30 КОП.

Сегодня—40-летие Ленинского комсомола

Да здравствует Всесоюзный Ленинский Коммунистический Союз Молодежи—верный помощник и резе Коммунистической партии, передовой отряд молод строителей коммунизма!

ЛЕНИНСКИЙ КОМСОМОЛ

В преддверии всенародного праздника—годовщины Великой Октябрьской социалистической революции—Советская страна отмечает 40-летие ВЛКСМ. Юбилей комсомола—это не только большой праздник сельского хозяйства, повышения культуры и благосостояния советских людей нашли горячую поддержку в комсомоле, еще более развили революционную энергию молодежи. Выполняя указания партии, комсо-

ШУМИХА РЕАКЦИОННОЙ ПРОПАГАНДЫ ВОКРУГ ЛИТЕРАТУРНОГО СОРНЯКА

Началами социалистического коллективизма проникнута вся жизнь советского общества. Давно на деле опровергнута лживая буржуазная легенда, будто социализм враждебен личности, будто он стирает и обезличивает индивидуальности и тормозит творческое развитие оригинальных людей и характеров. Напротив, именно при социализме, именно в атмосфере социалистического коллективизма создаются все условия для полнейшего развития творческой индивидуальности, для расцвета оригиналь-

Pravda, mouthpiece of the Kremlin, launches a furious attack on the author of *Dr Zhivago*

Communist Youth, Semichastny, called Pasternak, 'a swine which fouls its own trough'. He demanded the poet's expulsion from the Soviet Union.

The Writers' Association expelled Pasternak, declaring him to be unworthy of the title of 'Soviet Writer', and demanded that he be expelled from the homeland also. Not one of the poet's comrades or colleagues spoke in his defence, and perhaps this was a good thing. One trembles to think what would have happened if the 'Pasternak case' had grown into a palace revolution within the Writers' Association, and the one-sided abuse had become a political controversy. The die was cast anyway. The decision was no longer in the hands of the writers. Those amongst them whom the great epic poet Mikhail Sholokhov (the Association had wanted this man to receive the Nobel Prize) had called the 'dead souls' of the Writers' Association, willingly joined the chorus of abuse. But among those who now accused Pasternak were also to be found writers who themselves had had the courage to be critical during recent years. Among those who silently acquiesced

The *Literaturnaya Gazyeta* abuses him and publishes resolutions directed against him

were men of poetic genius who had endured the Stalin era with great dignity. It is not easy to say what they felt, but they were certainly more than mere willing tools who, at the slightest pressure, produced the required vilifications. Boris Pasternak, whom some of them had helped often enough, had, after all, always been a thorn in their flesh. Moreover they realized all too clearly that, by compromising, they had weakened their own creative work; and they had stifled their doubts and scruples again and again in the hope that these compromises would pave the way to a better future for their people. Now came a man who dared to state that it was not integration in a collectivist structure that mattered, but the preservation of the living, suffering individual. When this man accepted the award of the Swedish Academy, they had a reason to attack him, and to justify their own actions. By the light of their black-and-white reasoning Pasternak had become a renegade. They drowned the voice of their own uncertainty with the battle cry of the cold war. This is how the honour paid to the poet Pasternak became the 'Pasternak case'. But the propagandists, in both East and West, who wished to make a political scandal out of a great novel were, as events turned out, unmasked as petty and small-minded, as men whose narrow, utilitarian way of thinking prevented them from understanding a great human tragedy. With Boris Pasternak's letter to the most powerful man in the Soviet Union, however, the sequence of events, which had begun so hopefully with the award of the Nobel Prize, was taken out of the realm of politics once and for all, and raised to the heights of a great and moving human drama. The poet wrote to Khrushchev:

'Dear Nikita Sergeevich. I am addressing myself to you personally, to the Central Committee of the Soviet Communist Party, and to the Soviet Government. I have learned from the speech by Comrade Semichastny that the "government would put no difficulties in my way if I wished to leave the Soviet Union". For me to do this would be impossible. I am bound to Russia by my birth, my life and my work. I cannot imagine my fate separate from and outside Russia. Whatever my faults and mistakes may have been I could never have

The Soviet Minister of Culture, N. A. Mikhailov, at first had no objections to the award being made to Pasternak. But the organization, Komsomol, of which he was the leader, played a prominent part in the campaign against the poet

imagined that I should ever become the centre of a political campaign such as the one which has started in the West in connection with my name. Having realized this, I have informed the Swedish Academy of my voluntary renunciation of the Nobel Prize. For me to leave my country would be to die. I, therefore, ask you not to take this extreme measure against me. I can say, with my hand on my heart, that I have contributed to Soviet Literature, and that I can still be of use to it. B. Pasternak. October 31, 1958.'

Boris Pasternak has not been expelled from his country. He will live on in the land which he loves so deeply and so simply, even though this love is made so difficult for him.

The humiliations and threats which he had to endure are indescribable. His neighbours outdid the Press campaign against him with their vituperation. Demonstrators collected in front of his house, carrying posters with the inscription, 'Out, Judas!' People who had never read *Dr Zhivago* and for whom Pasternak the poet had no significance worked themselves up into hysterical fury. The police had to intervene, as it was feared that the demonstrators

Mikhail Sholokhov, the author of the novel *Quiet Flows the Don*, took strong exception to *Dr Zhivago* after the award

```
RS87

MOSCOU 40 29 1027 =


ELT MR ANDERS ACADEMIE DE SUEDE STOCKHOLM =



EN VUE DU SENS QUE CETTE DISTINCTION SUBIT DANS LA

SOCIETE QUE JE PARTAGE JE DOIS RENONCER AU PRIX IMMERITE

QUI MA ETE ATTRIBUE NE PRENEZ PAS EN OFFENSE MON REFUS

VOLONTAIRE
        PASTERNAK
```

Pasternak's telegram refusing the Nobel Prize

might storm the house, demolish it, or burn it down. Such illegal acts had to be prevented, in case they caused the international scandal to grow to an immense size. It was also important that Pasternak should not commit suicide.

The new holder of the Nobel Prize had to be prevented from going the same way as Mayakovsky and Yesenin. Special security precautions had to be taken. Doctors stood by. During those days the woman who had served as the model for *Lara*, again did her utmost to help Pasternak—in conversations and discussions in the Central Committee of the Party, in the Writers' Association, wherever there could have been the slightest hope. The worst

Even after the renunciation of the Nobel Prize Pasternak remained the object of bitter attacks

has indeed been averted. Boris Pasternak lives on—abused and expelled, but not broken; exhausted and ill, but with his will intact.

He, the great lyrical poet of Russia today, has proved that Maxim Gorky's words are still valid: 'The Russian poet is an indescribably lonely, tragically lonely figure.' When Gorky spoke these words he was thinking of the great Russian men of letters who exhausted their strength in a struggle with the spirit of their society and their time. Gorky's words are even more true today, because Russian poets are being denied even the right to be lonely, because of the constant demand for them to work according to the policy of the Party.

The officials of Red literature may say of Boris Pasternak's work that it is alien to Soviet literature. They may force that literature into uniformity, they may guide it, and falsify it. The country which produced Pushkin and Lermontov, Dostoyevsky and Tolstoy, Gogol and Chekhov, can never lose its human voice. That voice is not always loud and clear, but even in what the officials label as 'Soviet literature' it is never quite muffled by the false glitter of utilitarian political optimism.

The Russia whose art is courageous and ever-searching, dedicated to its own conscience and to the fate of all humanity, still lives, and will live for ever. The novel *Dr Zhivago* has suddenly opened the eyes of a world divided by ideological frontiers and cheap propaganda, to that other Russia for which Dostoyevsky raised his voice at the grave of Pushkin:

'I speak only of the brotherhood of man, not of the triumph of the sword, nor of the wonders of science, nor of grandiose economic achievements. For I am convinced that the heart of Russia, more than that of any other country, is dedicated to the world-wide union of all humanity.'

'Times will pass away. Many great times.

I shall no longer be there.

There will be no return to the days

of our fathers or our forefathers;

nor is this either necessary or desirable. ———

But that which is noble,

creative and great will, after a lengthy parting,

reappear at long last.

That will be an epoch of creativity.

Your life will then be at its fullest,

its most fruitful.

Remember me then.'

English rendering of dedication on opposite page

Zeiten werden vergehn. Viele grosse Zeiten. Ich
werde schon mehr nicht dasein. Es wird
keine Rückkehr zur Väter= oder Vorväter=
zeit sein, was auch doch nicht nötig und
wünschenswert ist. Aber das Edle, das Schöpfe-
rische und Grosse wird endlich wieder, nach
langem Scheiden, zum Vorschein kommen. Das
wird ein Ergebniszeitalter sein. Ihr Leben
wird dann am reichsten, am fruchtbarsten
sein. Gedenken Sie dann meiner.

Peredelkino.

B. Pasternak

A hand-written dedication of Boris Pasternak's

CHRONOLOGY

1890 February 10: birth of Boris Leonidovich Pasternak, first child of the Russian Jewish painter Leonid Pasternak and the pianist Rosa Kaufman-Pasternak, in Arsenal Street, Moscow.

1893 Leonid Pasternak is appointed to the headship of the Moscow School of Painting, Sculpture and Architecture. Removal to Myasnitsky Street. Birth of Boris's brother Alexander.

1900 First meeting with Rainer Maria Rilke while travelling to Yasnaya Polyana to visit Leo Tolstoy, a friend of the Pasternaks.

1901 After having been prepared for a German School in Moscow by his mother and tutors, Boris is accepted as a second-year pupil at the Humanist Gymnasium (Classical Grammar School) Number Five.

1903 Meeting with the composer Alexander Scriabin, Leonid Pasternak's neighbour at his country house in Obolenskoye. For the next six years Boris studies the theory of music.

1905 First meeting with Maxim Gorky. Manhandled by Cossacks at a demonstration during revolutionary unrest.

1906 First journey abroad with the family, to Berlin.

1907 Entry into the literary circle 'Serarda'. Pasternak attends debates on the birth of modern art in St Petersburg and Moscow. He is influenced by Scriabin's musical experiments and the exhibitions of surrealist, formalist and futurist works by young painters and sculptors. Contact with the neo-Kantian and symbolist intellectuals of the group round the periodicals *Musaget* and *Apollon*.

1908 Matriculation. First literary attempts. Private tutor to a wealthy industrialist's daughter, with whom he falls in love.

1909 Begins his legal studies at the Moscow University. On Scriabin's advice he changes to the study of philosophy. Gradual transition from music to literature.

1910 Discussion in the studio of the sculptor, Kracht, on the subject 'Symbolism and Immortality'. Death of Leo Tolstoy. Is present with other students when body of Tolstoy is transported to Yasnaya Polyana.

1911 Entry into the futurist literary group 'Centrifuge'.

1912 Work on his first volume of poems *The Twin in the Clouds*. Two hundred roubles, a present from his mother, finances his journey to Marburg in Germany. Begins his philosophic studies at the University of Marburg under Professors Hermann Cohen and Nikolai Hartmann. Summer journey to Switzerland and Italy.

1913 Return to Moscow. Final examinations at the University. Private tutor in the house of a German merchant living in Moscow.

1914 First encounter with the poet Mayakovsky in a literary debate. Is exempted from military service at the outbreak of the war on account of a leg injury incurred earlier. Tutor at the country estate of the poet

Baltrushaitis on the river Oka. Translates Kleist's *Der Zerbrochene Krug* (*The Broken Jug*) for the Moscow Kamerny Theatre production. His volume of poems *The Twin in the Clouds* is published.

1915 A year of travelling through Russia. Is employed in the management of the chemical factory at Uchkov in the Urals.

1916 Work on the volume of poems *Above the Barriers*.

1917 After the outbreak of the Revolution in Petrograd, journeys in a horse-drawn sledge from Uchkov to Moscow. Contact with the literary *avant garde*. *Above the Barriers* appears in Moscow. His translation of Kleist's *Der Zerbrochene Krug* appears in Gorky's periodical *The Contemporary*. Work on the volume of poems *My Sister, Life* and the short novel *The Childhood of Luvers*.

1918 Works as a librarian in the Soviet Ministry of Education during the Civil War and the literary-political struggle.

1921 His mother has serious heart trouble. Pasternak's parents and sisters go to Germany. They do not return to the Soviet Union but retain their Soviet citizenship. Boris and his brother Alexander remain in Moscow. Death of the poet, Alexander Blok, whom Boris Pasternak much admired.

1922 Death in Moscow of the futurist poet, Velemir Khlebnikov. Pasternak journeys with his finance, Evgenya, to Marburg and Berlin. Publication of his essay 'Observations on Art' in the periodical *Sovremennik*. His volume of poems, *My Sister, Life* is published in Berlin.

1923 Marriage to the Russian painter, Evgenya.

1924 His son, Evgeny is born. Publication of *The High Malady*, the short novel *The Childhood of Luvers*, and the collection of poems *Themes and Variations*.

1925 The Central Committee of The Communist Party of the Soviet Union publishes the 'Literary Manifesto'. December: Sergei Yesenin commits suicide in Leningrad. Work on *Aerial Ways*. Publication of Pasternak's *Stories*.

1926 Publication of a selection of poems, and the autobiographical epic poem *Spectorsky*.

1927 Pasternak makes unsuccessful attempts to come to terms with social and revolutionary problems of the day. The narrative poem *The Year 1905* is published.

1928 Mikhail Sholokhov publishes the first volume of his novel *Quiet Flows the Don*.

1931 After three years of silence, Pasternak's autobiographical prose work *Safe Conduct* is published. He is separated from his wife Evgenya and his son Evgeny. With his future wife, Zinaida Neyhaus, he visits Tiflis where they are guests of the Georgian poet Yashvili.

1932 Pasternak publishes his *Little Book for Children*, his collected stories *Aerial Ways*, and his short novel *The Childhood of Luvers* (in Leningrad). Publication of his volume of poems *Second Birth*.

1934 The Russian literary groups are dissolved. Foundation of the Soviet Writers' Association. Announcement of the Formula of Social Realism by the first Soviet Writers' Congress. The Party theorist, Nikolai Bukharin, praises Pasternak. First publication of the collected poems. Beginning of the poet's nine-year silence. Work on numerous translations: Georgian poetry, poems by Sandor Petoefi and Paul Verlaine, works by Goethe, Schiller, Kleist, Hervegh and the German Expressionists. Also works by Ben Jonson, Swinburne, Shelley and Shakespeare (*Hamlet, Othello, Macbeth, King Lear, Romeo and Juliet, Antony and Cleopatra*). Move to a country house in Peredjelkino near Moscow.

1935 Travels to Paris, via Berlin, as Russian delegate to the International Writers' Congress.

1936 Prince Mirsky, who had emigrated, returns to the Soviet Union and defends Pasternak.

1938 The literary paper *Literaturnaya Gazyeta* prints an extract from the continuation of the short novel *The Childhood of Luvers*. Purges in the Party and in writers' circles. Unsuccessful appeal to Stalin on behalf of the poet Osip Mandelstam who has been arrested. Birth of Pasternak's son Leonid. Execution of Nikolai Bukharin.

1941 Suicide of the poetess Maria Tsvetayeva, who had emigrated, but returned to the Soviet Union.

1943 Publication of the volume of poems *In Early Trains*, after a nine-year silence.

1944 The poem *Spring 1944* is published.

1945 Death of Boris Pasternak's father. Publication of the volume of poems *Wide Earth*. Attacked by the critics. Begins work on *Dr Zhivago*.

1946 On the orders of Andrei Zhdanov, special measures against several Soviet writers are instituted. The First Secretary of the Writers' Association, Aleksei Fadeyev, criticizes Pasternak's work.

Chronology 1948 Writers who had defended Pasternak are forced to indulge in self-criticism. Further work on *Dr Zhivago*.

1953 Stalin's death. Re-awakening of literary life. Publication of the translation of Goethe's *Faust*, Part One.

1954 Ten poems from the novel *Dr Zhivago* appear in the periodical *Znamya*. Attacked by the Soviet critics. Announcement that *Dr Zhivago* will be published in the summer.

1955 While on a visit to the U.S.A., the Soviet journalist, Victor Poltoratsky, attacks Pasternak. Pasternak translates Bertolt Brecht's speech of thanks on the award of the Stalin Peace Prize in Moscow.

1956 Pasternak's poems are published in periodicals and anthologies. May: Suicide of Aleksei Fadeyev. At the second plenary session of the Writers' Association Soviet youth is warned against Pasternak. The literary magazine *Novy Mir* rejects *Dr Zhivago*. The manuscript is submitted to the State Publishers for checking and cutting. In Milan the Communist publisher Giangiacomo Feltrinelli receives the copyright for an Italian edition.

1957 The Soviet authorities decide to proscribe the publication of *Dr Zhivago* in the Soviet Union. Pasternak appeals to the Italian publisher not to publish it. Attempts to intervene are made by the Secretary of the Soviet Writers' Association, Aleksei Surkov, and the Soviet Cultural Attaché in Milan. November 15: *Dr Zhivago* appears in Italian, published by Feltrinelli in Milan.

1958 Feltrinelli concludes agreements with eighteen publishers in Germany, England, America, Sweden and other non-Communist countries. *Dr Zhivago* wins the Bancarella Prize as the most successful book. October: Broadcasts by various radio stations in Western Germany of an adaptation of *Dr Zhivago* (by Ernst Schnabel). October 23: Award of the 1958 Nobel Prize for Literature to Boris Pasternak. He accepts the award. Attacks against Pasternak in the Soviet Press. He is expelled from the Soviet Writers' Association. October 28: *Dr Zhivago* appears in German. October 29: Pasternak finally renounces the Nobel Prize. Demands for his expulsion from the Soviet Union. The Moscow Writers' Association demands that he be deprived of Soviet citizenship. October 31: Pasternak addresses a letter to Khrushchev, then First Secretary of the Soviet Communist Party, and asks to be allowed to stay in Russia. November 6: In an article in *Pravda* Pasternak confesses his 'errors' and admits his 'guilt', November 7: Nehru criticizes the attacks on Pasternak.

NOTES ON THE PICTURES

2 Frontispiece: BORIS PASTERNAK

6 BORIS PASTERNAK'S PARENTS: the well-known painter and art teacher Leonid Pasternak (b. 1862 in Odessa, d. 1945 in Oxford) and Rosa Pasternak, née Kaufman (b. 1867 in Odessa). Until her marriage in 1889 Boris Pasternak's mother was a concert pianist, and a protegée of the celebrated Russian pianist Anton Rubinstein. In order to devote herself fully to her family Rosa Pasternak gave up her career as a musician in 1889. Painting by Leonid Pasternak. (Private coll.)

7 THE PASTERNAK CHILDREN—from left to right, Boris, Josephine, Lydia and Alexander—congratulating their parents on their Silver Wedding Anniversary in 1914. Painting by Leonid Pasternak (Private coll.)

8 THE EIGHT-YEAR-OLD BORIS, from a drawing by his father in 1898. This shows the boy at a time when his parents' friends and acquaintances were exercising a profound artistic influence upon the boy in Moscow (Ashmolean Art Museum, Oxford)

10 SERGEI RACHMANINOV (1873–1943), a portrait by Leonid Pasternak. At the time, Rachmaninov was world-famous as a virtuoso of the piano. After his studies in St Petersburg he lived in Moscow, but also stayed for a time in Germany and France. He was one of the closest friends of the Pasternak family until he left Russia. From 1919 onwards Rachmaninov lived in the U.S.A., where he died. (Private coll.)

11 ALEXANDER SCRIABIN (1872–1915). Boris Pasternak met the famous composer in 1902, when Scriabin was teacher of the pianoforte at the Moscow Conservatoire. As a result of this meeting with the brilliant musician, whose compositions contributed greatly to the development of harmonics in modern music, the boy's liking for music became a passion. From a drawing by Leonid Pasternak. (Private coll.)

12 LEO TOLSTOY (1828–1910). The poet—here seen in conversation with Vladimir Solovyev and Nikolai Fedorov—was a friend of the Pasternaks. Boris Pasternak always remembered him, and said of him, 'His spirit pervaded our whole house.' From a painting by Leonid Pasternak. (Private coll.)

13 TOLSTOY WORKING ON THE LAND. These sketches by Leonid Pasternak bring back memories of the visits paid by the Pasternaks to Yasnaya Polyana, the country estate of the great Russian poet. (Private coll.)

15 RAINER MARIA RILKE (1875–1926). The famous German poet's visit to Moscow in 1900, when Leonid Pasternak painted this portrait, was a great experience for the ten-year-old boy. Rilke's work later exercised a decisive influence on Boris Pasternak's lyric writing. (Private coll.)

16 BORIS AND ALEXANDER. Leonid Pasternak painted this portrait of his sons in 1905, the year of the first Russian revolution. (Private coll.)

17 MAXIM GORKY (1868–1936) was one of the great epic realists, who, in the second half of the nineteenth and at the beginning of the twentieth century, carried on the tradition of the classical Russian novel. The photograph is from the year 1910, when Gorky went abroad for a while. (Handke)

ANTON CHEKHOV (1860–1904) at first wanted to become a doctor, but soon after he had finished his studies he turned to writing. In his mature works—short stories, novels and plays—he characterized, with acumen and humour, men and women of his time, particularly from the lower middle classes and the landed gentry. (Ullstein)

18 THE REVOLUTION in 1905 was the first rebellion on the part of the simple, down-trodden Russian people against the feudal rule of the aristocracy and officialdom. When, on January 9, 1905, thousands of people gathered in St Petersburg in front of the Winter Palace to appeal to the Tsar for better living conditions, the Tsar ordered Cossack cavalry to attack the crowd and disperse it. On this 'Bloody Sunday' three thousand dead and wounded were left on the large square—victims of the blows and the rifle fire of the military. (Handke)

19 THE PRISON CHAPLAIN, GEORGI GAPON, led the protesting crowd to the Winter Palace in St Petersburg, but his entreaties fell upon deaf ears. (Ullstein)

21 BORIS PASTERNAK as a student (c. 1910). A drawing by his father, Leonid Pasternak. (Archives)

22 IN 1909 BORIS PASTERNAK was registered as a student of Law at Moscow University (founded 1755). But soon he changed over to the Faculty of Philosophy. Yet even there the lectures could not assuage his craving for knowledge. (AP)

23 LEO TOLSTOY ON HIS DEATH-BED, drawn in 1910 by Leonid Pasternak. The news of the death of Tolstoy, who had been an intimate friend of the Pasternak family, was a grave shock to Boris. (Private coll.)

24/5 THE ENTRY in the 'Students' Matriculation Register of the University of Marburg for the Summer Term 1912 (Faculty of Philosophy)' contains the following details: Pasternak, Boris; born 30. 1. 1890 in Moscow, Russia; Jewish; father: Professor at Art School in Moscow, resident at Volshonka Street, No. 14; documents: a Russian school certificate; registered 9. 5. 12, left 3. 8. 12. (Archives)

25 THE UNIVERSITY OF MARBURG, the first Protestant college, founded 1527, gave the town its character. When Boris Pasternak entered the University in 1912 the professorial chairs were held by men of great repute—Prof. Hermann Cohen and Nikolai Hartmann—whose fame went far beyond Germany's borders. (Lebeck)

26 HERMANN COHEN (1842–1918) was from 1876 until 1912 Professor of Philosophy at the University of Marburg. He was the founder and the leader of the 'Marburg School' of neo-Kantism. (Archives)

Nikolai Hartmann (1882–1950) was from 1909 Lecturer in Philosophy at the University of Marburg. When Boris Pasternak matriculated as a student, Hartmann still adhered to the neo-Kantian 'Marburg School', founded by Hermann Cohen. Later he developed his philosophical doctrine on the lines of a realist ontology. (Archives)

26 THE APARTMENT HOUSE IN MARBURG in which Boris lived as a student, stands in the Gysselbergstrasse, which, in *Safe Conduct*, Pasternak calls Giessener Street. (Lebeck)

27 THE YOUNG RUSSIAN STUDENT was deeply impressed by the narrow streets and the houses with their timber framework. Years later he wrote about these houses in *Safe Conduct*, 'Almost touching, they stretched out their hands towards each other across the road. There were no pavements in these alleys and some were closed to pedestrians.' (Lebeck)

29 AMONG THE CHURCHES OF ITALY, MILAN CATHEDRAL is second only to St Peter's in Rome in size. Built in white marble, it was begun in 1386, but was not completed till 1858. (Archives)

30/1 THE KREMLIN IN MOSCOW was in 1914, as it still is today, one of the most impressive sights of Russia's capital. (Handke)

32 BORIS PASTERNAK AND VLADIMIR MAYAKOVSKY met each other as literary antagonists during a discussion in a Moscow café. In spite of their divergent points of view on matters of art, they soon became friends. Pasternak, at that time, belonged to the extreme futurists among Russian lyric poets. (Private coll.)

33 CARICATURE OF VLADIMIR MAYA-KOVSKY (1894–1930), by Georges Annen-khov. At the beginning of his literary career he was a futurist. Later, he entirely devoted himself in his writing to the party-political day-to-day demands of the new regime. His poetry often managed to com-bine paeans of praise for new achievements with satirical comments about mismanage-ment. (Archives)

34 TSAR ALEXANDER III (1845–1894) suc-ceeded to the throne after the assassination of his father, Alexander II, in 1881. In the face of public opinion he adhered to the secret treaties made with Bismarck, and the power of the Tsarist regime was able to prevail once more. (Ullstein)

NICHOLAS II (1868–1918) was the last of the Russian Tsars. Heedless of the warning note sounded by the two uprisings in Odessa and in St Petersburg in 1905, which were put down with heavy loss of life, he continued on his harsh, feudal course. On March 15, 1917, he was forced to abdicate. Later he was arrested with all the members of his family by soldiers of the Red Army. On July 16, 1918, he was shot. (Handke)

34/5 MEETING OF THE WORKERS' AND SOLDIERS' COUNCILS in Petrograd in April 1917. They took over the reins in a Russia torn by revolution, and controlled parliament, the 'Duma'. (Handke)

36 DEMONSTRATIONS IN MOSCOW in the spring of 1917. The Army, which in 1905 had still loyally supported the Tsars, now lost all confidence in its leadership. In the years of bloody strife during the Revolution it was to split into various factions. (Wallis-furth)

37 ALEXANDER KERENSKY was one of the leading political personalities in the revolu-tionary turmoil of 1917. All his efforts to curb the Bolshevist revolution were un-successful, although he became Russian Prime Minister in July 1917, and even Generalissimo in September of the same year. (Ullstein)

38 REVOLUTION IN PETROGRAD. The troops, who were loyal to the government, could not withstand the onslaught of the Bol-shevist revolutionaries. They were shot down in the streets of Petrograd. The leader of the Government, Kerensky, managed to flee the country. (Wallisfurth)

39 THE STORMING OF THE WINTER PALACE in Petrograd was the climax of the bloody battles of the Revolution of 1917. With the capture of the Palace the centuries-old rule of the Tsars in Russia was finally

brought to an end. The Red Revolution had triumphed. (Ullstein)

40 ROSA PASTERNAK WITH HER DAUGHTERS at the piano. A drawing by Leonid Pasternak (1917). (Private coll.)

42 VLADIMIR ILYICH LENIN (in the background Josif Visaryonovich Stalin and Mikhail Ivanovich Kalinin) became, after the October Revolution, the new master of Russia. After an unsuccessful revolutionary attempt in July 1917 he had had to go into hiding in Finland, until the victorious revolutionaries set him up as the first head of the Soviet State on November 8, 1917. From a drawing by Leonid Pasternak (1921). (Private coll.)

43 BORIS PASTERNAK (c. 1920). Although the events of the Revolution concerned him greatly, he saw neither a catastrophe nor a victory in the assumption of power by the revolutionaries. He had no reason to emigrate, nor did he have any cause to praise the new regime. At that time his poetry had no political content. (Private coll.)

44 MAXIM GORKY (1868–1936). The great Russian writer, whose real name was Aleksei Maximovich Peshkov, made an early name for himself in his own country. His stories showed Marxist tendencies, and this led to persecution by the Tsarist authorities. In 1906, after a short period of imprisonment, he went abroad, but was allowed to return in 1913. After the Revolution he joined the Bolsheviks. In spite of his cultural-political functions in the young Soviet State, he often helped writers when they were threatened. When it was suggested to him that he should go abroad, he went to Berlin in 1921. Thence he retired to his villa in Sorrento. It was not until 1928 that he was able to return to the Soviet Union. (Historia Photo)

45 ALEXANDER BLOK (1880–1921) began by writing symbolist poems. Later, under the impact of the Revolution, he turned to more realistic subjects. He died in Leningrad in 1921, disillusioned by the results of the Revolution. (Ullstein)

46 SERGEI YESENIN (1895–1925). He and Mayakovsky were two of the best-known Russian poets of their time. Yesenin was able to express every human emotion in a language rich with images. He, too, for a short time thought that the events of the year 1917 held great promise. But later neither a world tour, nor his marriage to Isadora Duncan, could cure him of a fatal disillusionment and despair. He took his own life. (Archives)

47 VLADIMIR MAYAKOVSKY obeyed unhesitatingly the demands of the Revolution. He became the 'Drummer' and the 'Mouthpiece' of the Revolution, which he glorified in effusive poems. (Archives)

48 SERGEI YESENIN on a car trip with his wife, the dancer Isadora Duncan (1922). His poetic intoxication after the Revolution gave way to a bitter disappointment. He committed suicide in 1925. (Ullstein)

50 ROSA PASTERNAK, née Kaufman, the poet's mother, from a drawing by her husband, Leonid. Before her marriage she was a celebrated concert pianist. For years she suffered from serious heart trouble. Several times she went abroad to seek a cure for her illness. (Private coll.)

51 BORIS PASTERNAK'S PARENTS in Berlin. They left Russia in 1921, stayed for a time in Berlin, where his father, Leonid, gained a reputation, particularly as a portrait painter, and settled later in England. Leonid Pasternak died in Oxford in 1945. (Private coll.)

52 GUSTAV STRESEMANN (1878–1929), from a drawing by Leonid Pasternak. He was one of the leading politicians of the Weimar Republic. In 1918 he founded the 'Deutsche Volkspartei' (German People's Party); he became Chancellor of the Reich in 1923 and Foreign Minister in the same year, an office which he held until his death. Together with the French Foreign Minister, Aristide Briand, he was awarded the Nobel Peace Prize. (Private coll.)

ALBERT EINSTEIN (1879–1955). In 1914 he went from Zurich to Berlin where he was appointed Director of the Kaiser Wilhelm Institute of Physics. The great scientist, who, incidentally, loved to play the violin, was painted several times by Leonid Pasternak during his stay in Berlin. (Private coll.)

53 LEONID PASTERNAK, the poet's father, from a painting by Lovis Corinth. In Berlin the two painters, who were intimate friends, often sat for each other. This portrait, which Corinth painted in 1923, hangs in the Hamburg Kunsthalle. (Bruckmann)

54 BETWEEN WEST AND EAST: Fedor Mikhailovich Dostoyevsky, the author, *inter alia*, of *Crime and Punishment*, *The Idiot*, *The Brothers Karamasov*, one of the most important men in world literature, struggled, like so many Russian writers, with the vital problem of determining Russia's spiritual home. (Handke)

55 ALEXANDER PUSHKIN (1799–1837), from a drawing by Leonid Pasternak. He is regarded as the founder of modern Russian literature. His narrative in verse, *Eugene Onegin*, and his play, *Boris Godounov*, brought him world fame. Almost all later Russian poets were influenced by him. (Private coll.)

56 MAXIM GORKY (Aleksei Maximovich Peshkov: 1868–1936), renowned for his play *The Lower Depths* (1922) and several of his novels. Already in his early work he showed that he was a Marxist. In 1928 he returned to the Soviet Union, where he died on June 18, 1936, from pneumonia and weakness of the circulatory system which (allegedly on the orders of the OGPU chief, Nikolai Ivanovich Yeshov) was wrongly treated by the physician, Dr Levin. At that time the story that Gorky had been the victim of fascist agents was circulated in the Soviet Union. (Historia Photo)

57 STALIN AND BUKHARIN, after the death of Lenin (1924), determined the path which Russian literature was to take. The Party ideologist, Nikolai Ivanovich Bukharin, Professor at Moscow University (1888–1938), and with Lenin one of the leaders of the Revolution, was later executed on Stalin's orders. (Historia Photo)

58 VLADIMIR ILYICH LENIN (1870–1924). Even before his banishment from Russia (1902) he had prepared the downfall of the Tsarist regime. After the left wing of the Russian Social Democrats had, under his leadership, won the internal struggle for power against Kerensky, he was entrusted by the Workers' and Soldiers' Councils, in 1917, with the formation of a government. It took years, however, before Lenin, with the help of such friends as Bukharin and Kalinin, could establish himself firmly in his new position. After his death in 1924 the Soviet Union changed her political course. (Ullstein)

59 LEV DAVIDOVICH TROTSKY, born 1879, was murdered in Mexico on August 21, 1940. Lenin named Trotsky as his successor in his Will, which Stalin ordered to be altered. Stalin did not dare to liquidate

his dangerous rival at once, and so he exiled him from the Soviet Union. (Ullstein)

60 THE RUSSIAN REVOLUTION of 1905 began in Odessa. On June 14 of that year the seven hundred men of the crew of the battleship *Potemkin*, led by Naval Lieutenant Schmidt, joined forces with the dockers of Odessa who were on strike. These events on the battleship *Potemkin* play a symbolic role in Pasternak's epic poem *The Year 1905*. The uprising in Odessa was the subject of the excellent film, *The Battleship Potemkin*, by the famous Russian producer Eisenstein. (Handke)

61 LIEUTENANT SCHMIDT, the leader of the mutineer crew of the battleship *Potemkin*, in Odessa. (Historia Photo)

AS EARLY as 1917 Lieutenant Schmidt had become a legend. Revolutionaries named one of their tanks after him. (Wallisfurth)

62 'THE SPHINX'—the caricature (c. 1925) relates to Boris Pasternak, who, even then, was a well-known Russian lyric poet, and who eschewed politics and the struggle for power in literary circles. (Archives)

63 MAXIM GORKY back in Russia: in 1928, after an absence of seven years, he returned from Sorrento and was welcomed in Moscow by Bukharin and Khalatov, representing the Communist Party, and by a large crowd of people. As his creative author's voice was needed in Russia, he was treated with indulgence. (Historia Photo)

64 VLADIMIR MAYAKOVSKY committed suicide on April 14, 1930. Nevertheless, he was esteemed as one of the leading revolutionary writers even in later days. (Archives)

65 IN MOSCOW: Stalin, then General Secretary of the Communist Party of the Soviet Union, on his way to the Kremlin. After Lenin's death and Trotsky's banishment the dictator rid himself of troublesome rivals by the terrible 'purge trials'. Once he was dead, his methods were severely criticized by the Party. (Historia Photo)

67 BORIS PASTERNAK in the early 'thirties. His colleagues and friends did not survive the Stalin era and the time immediately following it. (dpa)

68 MAXIM GORKY, the 'friend of Stalin'. On his return to the Soviet Union the Party used him as a façade. (Historia Photo)

69 IN THE SADDLE—FOR THE TIME BEING: (from left to right) Rykov, Rlynov, Bukharin and Rudzutak. Rykov and Bukharin were shot on March 15, 1938.

70 JAMES JOYCE (1882–1941), the great Irish writer (*Ulysses*, 1922); John Roderigo Dos Passos (born 1896), the widely travelled American, who has had a great influence upon modern literature: Marcel Proust (1871–1922), the sensitive, introspective Frenchman: in the early 'thirties, after becoming once again subjects for discussion in the Soviet Union, they were condemned. The Party isolated Russia from the outside world. (Ullstein)

71 PASTERNAK'S PATRON: the Party theorist, Nikolai Bukharin, one of the most impressive personalities of the new Russia, who at first supported Pasternak. (AP)

72 ANDRE MALRAUX (real name, Berger, born November 3, 1901), French writer, General and politician, whom Pasternak avoided meeting when he visited Paris in 1935 as a delegate to the International Writers' Congress. Malraux, who fought on the side of the Insurgents in the Spanish

Civil War and during the revolution in China, turned against the Communists in 1947. (Camera-Press)

73 JEAN COCTEAU, born 1892, has made a name for himself through his books and his films. Pasternak avoided him, too, during his stay in Paris in 1935 as a delegate to the Writers' Congress. (UP)

74 THE WAR with Germany brought, for a time, a certain relaxation of controls, both mental and physical, in the Soviet Union. All forces in the Soviet Union, Communist and non-Communist, joined in fighting the invaders. Twice the war swept across Russian towns and villages, which suffered almost total destruction. (Archives)

75 THE TEMPORARY TRUCE: while the war lasted the struggle for power yielded to the great national task of successfully repelling the German attack. Russia sent millions of soldiers to the front. (Archives)

76/7 AFTER THE VICTORY: in 1945 the war came to an end. The Red Army occupied large parts of Germany. In celebration of their victory the Red Army erected many large memorials. (This statue of Stalin in Budapest resembles the monuments in Russia.) (AP)

78 BORIS PASTERNAK after the war. The Party once more tightened the reins. In 1945 Pasternak began to work on his novel *Dr Zhivago*. (Keystone)

80 ANDREI ZHDANOV (born on February 26, 1892) who was considered Stalin's successor, died on August 31, 1948. In 1939, Zhdanov, the defender of Leningrad, joined the Political Bureau of the Party, and in 1947 became the head of the Cominform, of which he himself was the founder. For years, as the leading Party ideologist, he determined what the artistic life of Russia should be. (Archives)

81 ILYA EHRENBURG, winner of the Stalin Prize in 1947, was born on January 27, 1891. He is one of the most striking personalities in Soviet 'literary politics'. In 1954 he published his important novel *The Thaw*. (dpa)

82 THE MOSCOW ARTS THEATRE was founded in 1898 as a repertory theatre by Stanislavsky and Nemirovich-Danchenko. The present board of directors (from left to right: Solodovnikov, Stanitsin and Raevsky), who perpetuated the 'naturalist' style favoured by the founders of the theatre, produced several plays by Shakespeare, Goethe and Schiller, as rendered into Russian by Boris Pasternak. (Keystone)

83 ALEKSEI FADEYEV, for many years Pasternak's neighbour in Peredjelkino, was First Secretary of the Soviet Writers' Association. He had been a full member of the Central Committee of the Communist Party in the Soviet Union, but after the 20th Congress of the Party he was reduced to the rank of candidate member. Fadeyev, who gave the Party his full support as a poet, committed suicide in May 1956. (dpa)

84 KONSTANTIN STANISLAVSKY (K. S. Alekseyev, 1863–1938) and Vladimir Ivanovich Nemirovich-Danchenko (1858–1943) in 1888 founded the Society for Art and Literature from which, a year later, grew the Moscow Arts Theatre. Their productions were models of 'naturalist' stagecraft. (Keystone)

85 IN THE DRAMA THEATRE in Moscow many European classics, translated by Pasternak, were performed, among them Schiller's *Kabale und Liebe* (*Love and Intrigue*) with L. P. Bogdanova in the part of Louise, and N. D. Nicomarov in that of President von Walter. (Zentralbild/Tass)

86 THE TRIUMVIRATE, Malenkov, Bulganin and Khrushchev in Moscow during the anniversary celebrations of the October Revolution (1954). On March 5, 1953, after Stalin's death, they took over the government. From that day on, everyone in the Soviet Union looked forward to a more liberal way of life. (UP)

86/7 IN THE KREMLIN MAUSOLEUM, the national shrine of the Soviet Union, Lenin and Stalin lie in state, side by side. (Archives)

88 THE WRITER ILYA EHRENBURG, the Armenian painter Saruyan, and the bearded sculptor Konenko give a Press conference in Moscow. (Wallisfurth)

89 PASTERNAK and his second wife, Zinaida, in their country house in Peredjelkino. (Private coll.)

90 IN 1955 THE GERMAN PLAYWRIGHT BERTOLT BRECHT received the Stalin Peace Prize in Moscow. He asked Pasternak to translate his speech of thanks into Russian. At a ceremony in Moscow the Russian poet N. S. Tikhinov, who was the president of the Soviet Peace Committee, handed the Soviet prize to Brecht.

91 HELENE WEIGEL, Brecht's widow, in 1957 gave a performance in Moscow with the 'Berlin Ensemble'. Pasternak, who previously had not thought much of Brecht's work, revised his judgement after having seen the play *The Caucasian Chalk Circle*. After the performance Helene Weigel, who was a great success, signed autograph books. (Keystone)

92 VLADIMIR DUDINTSEV'S novel *Not By Bread Alone*, published in 1956, attracted great attention all over the world. This sensitive and strong-willed writer was sharply reprimanded by the Party. (Archives)

THE RENEWED HARDENING of policy in the Soviet Union, and the rebuking of many poets by the Soviet Writers' Association, was on various occasions the subject of cartoons in the Moscow satirical magazine *Krokodil*. (*Krokodil*)

93 KONSTANTIN FEDIN (b. 1892), Pasternak's neighbour in Peredjelkino, in 1956 protested against the publication of *Dr Zhivago*. In his own novels Fedin glorified the Communist revolution. (dpa)

95 AFTER THE UPRISING in Hungary in November 1956 the period of liberalization was finally over. Under fire from Russian tanks in Budapest thousands of Hungarians died, and so did the hopes of many where the Soviet Union was concerned. (Weitz)

96 ALEKSEI ALEXANDROVICH SURKOV, Stalin Prize winner and member of the Supreme Soviet, was born in 1899. Surkov, who had taken part in the Civil War, and is currently the chief editor of the magazine *Orgonyol*, wrote a large number of war books which made him extremely popular in the Soviet Union. In 1957, as the First Secretary of the Soviet Writers' Association, he tried in vain to prevent the publication of the Italian edition of Pasternak's novel *Dr Zhivago*. 'Pasternak is my ideological enemy,' he recently told a British reporter. 'If I had my way, I should turn him out of the country.' (Ullstein)

97 THE MILAN PUBLISHER Dr Giangiacomo Feltrinelli, until recently a wealthy member of the Italian Communist Party, was not to be deterred by appeals or threats from publishing *Dr Zhivago* in Italian. The book appeared on November 15, 1957. A year later, Feltrinelli signed contracts with publishers in eighteen non-Communist countries.

98 PASTERNAK'S 'DACHA' (country house) in the writers' colony at Peredjelkino near Moscow. The house was put at his disposal by the Soviet Writers' Association in 1934. (Private coll.)

99 BORIS PASTERNAK, winner of the Nobel Prize, outside his 'dacha'. (Capa-Magnum)

100 BORIS PASTERNAK, working at his desk. (Magnum)

103 VISITORS TO PEREDJELKINO. Boris Pasternak entertains at his home. (dpa/Capa-Magnum)

104/5 THE CHANGING FACE OF MOSCOW. The Soviet Union's determination to expand and develop shows itself nowhere so clearly as in the imposing façade of Moscow. Whole districts of the capital were pulled down to make way for the architectural designs of the Soviet town planners. (Wallisfurth)

106 THE SATIRICAL MOSCOW MAGAZINE *Krokodil* often ridiculed Soviet writers, who, after Stalin's death, were made to feel insecure by the fluctuations of the Party's policy. (*Krokodil*)

107 A CARICATURE, directed against Pasternak: 'This is a clean job!' says the editor of a Western 'rag' about the novel *Dr Zhivago*. With such cartoons the Soviet Press reacted to the success of the novel in the non-Communist world. (*Krokodil*)

108 FELTRINELLI, the Italian publisher of *Dr Zhivago*, with copies of the book in various languages. Its success in the West has been phenomenal, partly due to the controversy over the Nobel Prize award, but also on its own merits. (Keystone)

109 KHRUSHCHEV, on learning of the success of *Dr Zhivago* outside the Soviet Union, toyed with the idea of sending Pasternak to Baku so that he could write about the oilfield workers there.

110 ALBERT CAMUS, French winner of the Nobel Prize for Literature in 1957, was born in 1913. As early as the Spring of 1958, he considered Pasternak to be the most likely candidate for the Nobel Prize. (UP)

111 AFTER A GRAVE ILLNESS: Boris Pasternak in Peredjelkino in the Spring of 1958. (Private coll.)

112 THE NOBEL PRIZE COMMITTEE of the Swedish Royal Academy in Stockholm, which, on October 23, 1958, awarded the Nobel Prize for Literature to Pasternak for his poetry and his novel *Dr Zhivago*. (AP)

113 IVAN ALEKSEYEVICH BUNIN (1870–1953), a writer of Russian lyric and epic poems, emigrated from the Soviet Union in 1933. His novel *Arsenyev's Life* was largely autobiographical. He was the first Russian writer to receive the Nobel Prize for Literature. (dpa)

114 EVEN before the Swedish Royal Academy had made its final decision, congratulatory letters and telegrams reached Pasternak in Peredjelkino. On the morning of October 23, 1958, a foreign radio station announced in a broadcast that Pasternak was the most likely person to win the Nobel Prize. (dpa)

115 ENTHUSIASTIC FRIENDS, among them the poet Nikolai Chukovsky, congratulate Pasternak on his award. (Capa-Magnum)

116 WESTERN CORRESPONDENTS, wishing to interview the new Nobel Prize winner, found Pasternak in the garden of his 'dacha' in Peredjelkino. (Capa-Magnum)

Notes on the Pictures

117 THE ATTACKS of the Russian Press on the Nobel Prize winner occupied the headlines in the non-Communist newspapers for many days. The West was almost unanimously on Pasternak's side.

118 THE MOSCOW NEWSPAPER *Pravda* made vicious attacks upon the author of *Dr Zhivago*. These attacks stirred up hatred against the man who had refused to allow himself to be regimented. (*Pravda*, 29. 10. 1958)

119 THE CAMPAIGN against Pasternak was opened by the literary paper *Literaturnaya Gazyeta*, the official organ of the Soviet Writers' Association. In column after column the paper published resolutions against the Nobel Prize winner. (*Literaturnaya Gazyeta*, 25. 10. 1958)

120 THE SOVIET MINISTER OF CULTURE, N. A. Mikhailov, at first had no objection to the choice made by the Nobel Prize Committee. However, the youth organization 'Komsomol', of which he was the leader, took a particularly active part in the campaign against Pasternak. (Zentralbild)

121 MIKHAIL SHOLOKHOV, great epic poet and author of the novel *Quiet Flows the Don* (1928–1940), was born on May 24, 1905. It was he whom the Soviet Writers' Association consider should have received the Nobel Prize for 1958. Sholokhov willingly joined in the chorus of abuse against Pasternak. Even when the leader of the Young Communists, Semichastny, consumed with hatred, called Pasternak a 'swine which fouls its own trough', Sholokhov remained silent. (dpa)

122 THE TELEGRAM, dated October 29, 1958, with which Boris Pasternak renounced the Nobel Prize. Addressed to the Permanent Secretary of the Swedish Royal Academy, it reads: 'In view of the interpretation of this distinction in the community to which I belong, I must give up this undeserved prize which has been awarded to me. Please do not look upon my voluntary refusal with ill-feeling. Pasternak.' (AP)

123 IN SPITE OF PASTERNAK'S renunciation of the Nobel Prize, there were demands for his banishment from the Soviet Union. On October 31, 1958, he wrote to Khrushchev, asking to be allowed to remain in Russia. (Archives)

124 BORIS PASTERNAK'S HAND-WRITING, from a dedication written in German. (Private)

140

INDEX OF NAMES